ANGELS

ANGELS

THE MYTHOLOGY OF ANGELS AND THEIR EVERYDAY PRESENCE AMONG US

CHARLOTTE MONTAGUE

CHARTWELL
BOOKS, INC.

CONTENTS

INTRODUCTION

Since ancient times, the human race has believed in the existence of angels. At different periods in history and across many cultures, angels have been represented as heavenly beings carrying messages of hope, joy and comfort from the spiritual world to those suffering hardship, loss or distress. Today, that belief appears to be as strong as ever, despite the decline, in many countries, of organized religious faith.

WHAT IS AN ANGEL?

Angels are traditionally seen as winged creatures, half human in form (either male or female), emitting a dazzling light, and being very beautiful to behold. Whether in Judaism, Christianity, or Islam, stories are told of angels appearing in visions, especially to holy men and women, and imparting the word of God. The most famous of these, of course, is the story of the Annunciation, in which the Archangel Gabriel appears to Mary to tell her that she will become the mother of Christ.

That said, many great religious teachers, from the fifth-century John Chrysostom to the medieval scholars Moses Maimonides and St Thomas Aquinas, have taught that this concept of the angel – as a beautiful, winged half-human creature appearing in a vision – is a somewhat over-literal one, designed to explain the mysteries of God's nature to uneducated people. According to them, the angel is not a real being, but a personification of the divine, represented in human form to indicate its relation to the earthly world. In their view, the angel's wings, and its halo, are representations by artists that are put there to mark it out from ordinary mortals, and show that it is essentially a spiritual being. However, they should not be taken too literally.

The Non-literal View

The Judaic, Christian, and Islamic scriptures tell of a complex hierarchy of angels. For example, in Christianity, angels are ranked in order from the highest (the archangels) to the lowest (the guardian angels). In the same way, the Jewish hierarchy ranges from the Chayot, who stand nearest to God, to the Ishim, who are like men, and are cited in the Kaballah as 'the beautiful souls of just men'. Over the centuries, scholars from many faiths have tended to interpret these different classes of angels as revealing the many aspects of God's nature, rather than as a literal run-down of what to expect when we reach heaven. As Maimonides says in his philosophical work, *The Guide for the Perplexed*, 'When man sleeps, his soul speaks to the angel, and the angel to the cherub'. He believed that angels were created by God to carry messages to humanity, taking on human form to present revelations in a way that ordinary people could understand, rather than being actual physical entities. For this reason, Maimonides and other scholars, whether Jewish, Christian, or Islamic, emphasized that angels themselves should not be worshipped.

In the same way, the Christian mystic St Thomas Aquinas thought of angels as beings of the intellect, who mirrored the perfection of God and the universe. According to him, angels have no physical bodies, but sometimes assume the form of human beings to communicate with us on earth. For Aquinas, angels represent the ultimate in what might be possible for humans to achieve in terms of love and understanding.

The Annunciation to the Shepherds: detail of the angel, by Nicolaes Pietersz. Berchem, 1656.

Communication With Angels

It is this idea of angels as non-literal beings who exist to bring us messages of love, understanding, and companionship from a higher spiritual realm, that seems to appeal so greatly to us in the modern world. Whether in religious texts, in newspaper articles, in books, on the internet, or from everyday anecdotes that we hear from friends and relatives, there are literally hundreds of stories about ordinary people – sometimes religious believers, sometimes not – who have had contact with angels. These angels may appear in many guises: an angel may speak to us as a voice in our heads, make its presence felt in a room (whether through a slight breeze or a feeling of light and warmth), or be sensed through the words and actions of a kind stranger. In this book, you will find many such stories, some of them famous, some of them obscure.

Today, centuries after the teachings of the medieval scholars mentioned above, this is how we most often think of the angel: not so much as a heavenly beings with wings, a halo, and a white gown, who appears before us in a vision, but as a comforting spiritual presence that may come to us in our time of need, to help restore our faith, and to lend us the energy to take on the difficult tasks of life.

Belief in Angels Today

Indeed, in the new millennium, far from being relegated to the realms of mythology, the angel has become more popular than ever. According to a poll recently conducted by *Time* magazine, over 50% of Americans today believe in angels, and of these, 46% are convinced that they have a guardian angel taking a personal interest in their wellbeing. One in five of those questioned also noted that they did not think of themselves as religious. Commentators have also noted that significantly more Americans believe in the existence of angels than in global warming,

since the figure of those who believe in global warming stands at only 36%. In addition, 68% of Americans believe that angels and demons are active in the world today.

In the wake of the atrocities of 9/11, many Americans believed that evil forces were at work, in the shape of an 'angel of death' that could be seen outlined in the smoke pouring out of the twin towers of the World Trade Center. The office workers who jumped out of windows and fell to their death were seen as 'fallen angels', while those who selflessly went to help others were considered to be angels in human guise. In the same way, survivors of terrorist attacks and disasters around the world, whether fires, bombings, or accidents, often tell of an unknown stranger appearing and leading them to safety, whom they later understand to be an angel (either literally or metaphorically). Such stories surround the London bombings of 7 July 2005, the Bangkok nightclub fire of 1 January 2009, and the Chile mining disaster of 5 August 2010. Whether we believe them or not, in literal terms, we can remember the wisdom of Aquinas: that the image of the angel is there to remind us that we are sometimes capable of reaching our human aspiration towards kindness, selflessness, love, and companionship – in short, to show us how we can aim to be better than we are.

Angel Sightings

In the UK, a study made in 2002 detailed experiences of over 200 people who said that their experiences of angels consisted of the following: seeing visions, sometimes with multiple witnesses present; hearing voices, for example to convey warnings; a sense of being touched, pushed, or lifted to avert a dangerous situation; and smelling a pleasant fragrance, usually in the context of a loved one's death. In a survey of teenage beliefs, 78% of those interviewed said that they believed in angels, while it was found that belief in other supernatural phenomena, such as the Loch Ness

Monster or extra-sensory perception, had largely declined. Thus, we can see that the concept of the angel is still a powerful one today, especially among a rising generation of young people.

Channelling the Angel

A host of websites and numerous books bear witness to this growing belief in angels, and in this book we delve into how believers may connect with the spirit world. Via the traditional route of praying, we look at creating the perfect environment to initiate contact through the construction of an angel altar – a special area dedicated to communication with angels. At the altar, meditation, visualization and letter writing are practised, along with crystal therapy. The types of crystals needed for crystal therapy are detailed in this book, along with the powers associated with the various colours. Angels can activate crystals and they can then be used as tools for healing, a practice which is very popular in alternative medicine as well as for communing with the spirit realm. The use of essential oils is explored, as well as the power of colours for attracting angels, whether in our clothing or as a decorative

The Angel and the Mother, by Louis Janmot, 1854.

element in our angel altar. Angel cards, or oracle cards, are frequently used in much the same way as tarot cards. We use these to ask questions, and we ask the angels to answer through the cards we turn over or pick. Another method an angel may use to communicate with us is by sending us signs. These can be sent to us while we are sleep, or during the day. These signs are often slightly obscure or symbolic, but sometimes can be blatant messages, such as advice in the form of a newspaper headline or a song on the radio. These methods of communication are often used by those that believe in our heavenly helpers, but there are other ways to keep the angels near without creating an altar or buying crystals. Many online shops and retail outlets offer the equivalent of the medieval 'relic' – items such as 'pocket angels' made of crystal or semi-precious stone, that we can carry with us to access the spiritual world of the angel whenever we need to, whether for assistance, advice, or simply as a kind of modern-day talisman. Some may argue that this trade is essentially commercial; however, it is clear that many people derive comfort and pleasure from these harmless trinkets, as has been the case throughout human history.

THE NEW AGE MOVEMENT

One of the most important forces behind the recent surge of non-denominational, and sometimes non-religious, belief in angels today is the New Age movement, which developed in the latter half of the 20th century. The movement takes its name from the radical poet William Blake, himself a visionary who told of seeing angels from childhood. Blake had faith that there would be a utopian 'new age' to come, sweeping away the gross commercialism and horrifying poverty of his own era and replacing it with a more harmonious existence akin to that of the biblical Garden of Eden. This very general, inclusive movement draws on many Eastern and Western belief systems to create a holistic spirituality that focuses on personal growth and self-help, rather than insisting on outmoded religious dogma. Its critics accuse the movement of lacking scientific rigour or religious commitment, but there is no doubt that it holds a powerful appeal for those who reject the traditional teachings of the established religions while seeking to retain some spiritual belief system in their lives.

The Ancient Religions

Significantly, the New Age movement draws on many pre-Christian religions, taking inspiration from ancient religions in which there were many gods, such as shamanism (the belief in good and evil spirits that can be controlled only by rituals carried out by a holy person) and animism (the belief that animals have souls). In these early religious cultures, people worshipped natural phenomena, such as trees, stars, rivers, rain, crops, and so on. They also believed that they should live in harmony with birds and animals, which were thought to be as powerful as human beings.

In those days, of course, primitive hunter-gatherers and early farmers were at the mercy of the elements, and so believed that the spirits of the earth and the animals that gave them sustenance must be revered and respected – not such a foolish belief, as it now turns out, centuries later, as our planet struggles to survive the onslaught of global technology.

Nature Spirits and Angels

Over the course of human history, we can trace how these 'polytheistic' beliefs – belief in many gods or spirits – gave way to 'monotheism', the belief in one God alone. In a sense, this was to do with the increasing power of man over nature (for example in Egyptian civilization, whose architects found a way to harness the power of water by using the Nile to irrigate land).

Little by little, as human civilizations gained more and more control over the earth's resources through advancing technology, their rulers began to believe that they no longer had to appease the spirits of nature, but could actually begin to manage the natural world to their advantage, in a rational way. However, instead of rejecting the ancient nature gods and goddesses altogether, which would have been very unpopular among the deeply superstitious ordinary folk, the pioneers of the new monotheistic religions, whether Judaism, Christianity, or Islam, found a way of incorporating them into the religious hierarchy: as angels.

In Zoroastrianism, dating from the 10th century BC, that the spirit of light, Ahura Mazda, is elevated from being one among many spirits, to being the central deity. All the other deities, apart from the spirit of darkness, or evil, are demoted to the status of 'archangels' ('Amesha Spentas'), 'adorable ones' ('Yatazas'), or 'guardian angels' ('Fravishis'), becoming secondary characteristics, abstract aspects, or lesser versions of Ahura Mazda. In this way, the prophet Zoroaster tried to move towards belief in one God, and a modern, moral universe in which Good and Evil were the prime movers, while still retaining a place for the ancient spirits that people had worshipped for centuries in Iran.

Fire and Wind: Seraphim and Cherubim

In early Judaic teachings, we find a similar process taking place. Here, the spirits worshipped by the early Semitic tribes reappear as angels. The ancient spirit of fire becomes the class of angel known as the Seraphim (literally, in Hebrew, the 'burning ones'). The storm or wind deity transforms into the Cherubim, described as 'the wings of the wind'. Other elements of the belief systems of the early Semitic tribes also survive in the Judaic hierarchy of angels, including the worship of the bull (the Shedu) or the lion (the Lammasu), both of which are represented with wings and a human head. In Eastern religions such as Buddhism and Hinduism, we also find elements of folk belief that find their way into the faith, for example with the Garuda, a bird-like creature that brings nectar from heaven to those on earth. Ancient pagan faiths also have their share of angel-like icons, such as the Norse Valkyries and the Celtic fairies.

The Angel Journey

Here we uncover a strange journey, in which the ancient pagan spirits of light, fire, wind, and so on went on to find a new existence as angels in the major world religions. In view of this, it is fascinating to see how the angel continues to appeal to the modern-day spiritual believer. It is as if the wheel has turned full circle: in ancient times, the spirits were worshipped as the essence of woods, rivers, trees, and other natural phenomena. These spirits were then incorporated into the main monotheistic religions as angels, saints, and other lesser beings serving a central God. Now, however, through the teachings of the New Age movement, which reject the idea of a central deity, the focus has reverted to the spirits once more, in the shape of a renewed interest in angels as the messengers from a higher spiritual plane, but also embodying the spirits of nature as in the ancient days.

In this book, you can find out about that journey, whether in history, religion, art, literature, popular culture, or as a matter of everyday ritual, belief, and practice. Here, we explore the breathtaking array of ideas, experiences, and representations of the angel, throughout human history, at many different times, and in many different cultures. In this way, we hope that you can perhaps begin to understand just how important the angel as a symbol of hope, companionship, love, and strength has been to humanity across the ages, and continues to remain to this day.

ANGEL ENCOUNTERS

Chilean Mining Disaster

Angels make many appearances in the legends that surround news stories today. One of the most extraordinary of these is that of the 'butterfly angel' who helped save the lives of the Chilean miners trapped underground after the Copiapo accident of 2010.

The 'Butterfly Angel'

The mine is situated in the Atacama Desert and had a poor safety record, having been unstable for many years. On 5 August 2010, it collapsed, leaving 33 men trapped over 2,000 feet below ground. Eventually, after a gruelling period of 69 days spent underground, all the men were rescued. During this time, their families and friends set up a small settlement at 'Camp Hope' nearby, sending messages of support to the men while they waited to be rescued.

The Collapse of the Mine

At night, the families would huddle round the fire and tell stories to keep up their spirits. One of these was the tale of Jorge Galeguillos, one of the men trapped down in the mine. While he was underground, Galeguillos wrote a letter to his brother Eleodoro, telling of the events that led to the accident. He told how when the accident happened, deep down in the mine, he was a passenger in a pick-up truck driven by a friend, Franklin Lobos, a former football star. As they drove along, a slab of rock crashed down onto the road behind them, missing the car by seconds.

Ahead of them, Jorge noticed a small white butterfly. It was so unusual to see a butterfly down in the mine that he and his friend slowed down the truck, stopping to take a look at it. Had they not done so at that very moment, they would have driven straight into the area where the tunnel collapsed, and would definitely have been killed in the tons of rubble that came crashing down.

The two friends were caught in a great avalanche of dirt and dust, which blinded them for some time. Around them, they could feel the tunnel collapsing, blocking the mineshaft between two of the levels, which set off a series of smaller rock falls further down. It must have been a terrifying experience, and one that the miners will ever forget. However, Jorge and Franklin managed to drive to safety, finding their way around the rubble blocking large parts of the tunnel, until they reached the 31 other miners trapped on another level, in a safety zone only 50 square metres wide.

A Guardian Angel?

The miners later speculated as to how a white butterfly could find itself 500 metres below the earth. They began to wonder whether they had seen a guardian angel, who had led them to safety. Like most people in the area, Galeguillos was a devout Catholic, and had a strong belief in guardian angels. In addition, he was familiar with the folklore of the region, which was full of stories about white animals bringing good luck, especially if seen at night. Thus, a combination of religion and superstition led him to believe that he had been singled out and rescued by a being from on high, through God's will.

Jorge's brother Eleodoro was also convinced that the butterfly was an angel warning them of danger, and telling them to avoid it. Undoubtedly, the appearance of the butterfly saved the lives of the two men, who would have been buried alive had it not danced before them, intriguing them so much that they stopped to look, and thus avoided being crushed to death.

A Miracle from God

To date, no scientific explanation has been offered as to how a butterfly could have flown so far underground into the mine. It is known that when flowers bloom in the desert, small white butterflies are sometimes seen nearby. However, the nearest patch of blossom was over two kilometres away from the mine.

It is thought by some that perhaps the butterfly could have been sucked into the mine down a ventilation chimney when the tunnel collapsed, but such an event seems rather unlikely. From the religious Chilean miners' point of view, the butterfly was a miracle, a sign of God's help, in that it led the two men to safety.

Jorge Galeguilos was not the only miner to believe that the events of 5 August had a religious significance. One of the others trapped, Mario Sepulveda, believed that the accident represented a turning point in his life: 'I was with God and the Devil,' he said later, 'and God took me'. Monica Avalos, the wife of the first man to be rescued, Florencio Avalos, believed that God was present throughout the ordeal, and that the rescue that took place was nothing short of a miracle. Her sentiments were echoed by the Chilean president, Sebastian Pinera, who said, 'When the first miner emerges safe and sound, I hope all the bells of all the churches of Chile ring out with joy and hope. Faith has moved mountains.'

A screen grab of an unidentified miner trapped in San Jose mine in Copiapo, Chile.

Chilean miner, Florencio Avalos, comes out of the Fenix
capsule after being brought to the surface on 12 October 2010.

SANTIKA NIGHTCLUB

One of the most fascinating stories of an angel coming to the rescue concerns a fire at the Santika nightclub in Bangkok, Thailand. The fire broke out as the clock struck midnight on new years' eve 2008, killing 66 people and injuring over 200 others. Ironically, the band playing on stage at the time were named Burn.

The Santika nightclub was a popular hotspot for holidaymakers and because of this most of the victims were tourists, from Australia, Europe, the US, Canada, and the Far East. It is unclear what caused the fire – some allege that it was the result of a pyrotechnics display on stage, some claim the sparklers given to revellers at midnight started the fire – but it seems that, whatever the reason, safety concerns were not a priority in the club. The wiring was unsound, the building materials in the roof makeshift, and there was only one exit door available for use – there were in fact, two more doors in the building, but one was locked to prevent robberies, and another was known only to the club's staff. Bars across windows prevented them being used as an escape route, and there were no emergency procedures in place in the event of a fire.

In addition, the cheap plastics used to waterproof the roof caused toxic smoke when they began to burn. As a consequence of this lack of attention to safety, not only did the building catch fire very quickly, burning and suffocating many victims within a matter of minutes, but others were also seriously injured in the stampede to escape.

The Voice of an Angel

One of the revellers that night, Alex Wargacki, aged 29, worked as a foreign trader in Bangkok, and had lived there for four years. He was originally from Finchley, North London. When the fire broke out, he scrambled towards the exit, along with around a thousand other clubbers. However, the door was very small, and a crowd of people were jammed up against it, making it impossible for him to get out. He searched for another way out, but found all the windows barred. The flames grew higher, from floor to ceiling, and he could hear the noise of the windows cracking as they became consumed by the fire. Unable to escape, the flames and fumes overcame him, and he struggled for breath, aware that there was no oxygen in his lungs. He fell to the floor and lost consciousness.

The next thing he knew was that as he woke up, he heard a voice say to him, 'come on, come this way'. He felt a hand clasp his, and then he was dragged towards an exit. A crowd of people parted to let him out. Outside, he felt the cool of the night air, and was able to breathe again.

To this day, he does not know who his rescuer was, but he believes that it could have been an angel. He resolved while he was in hospital being treated for burns and lung damage, that he would never forget the angel that saved his life.

A police officer guards the scene of the Santika nightclub fire.

THE SOVIET COSMONAUTS

In 1985, an angel sighting was reported from space, aboard the *Salyut 7*, the final space station to be launched in the Soviet Union's programme. The station experienced various technical failures during its period of eight years and two months in space, and was visited by 10 crews while in orbit.

On one occasion during their stay at the station as it orbited earth, Cosmonaut Vladimir Solevev and his colleagues Oleg Atkov and Leonid Kizim noticed an extraordinary sight. Seven giant figures approached the station, all of them winged, and looking like human beings. On each of their heads was a ring of mist, like a halo. They were struck by the fact that these celestial beings, as they called them, looked exactly like biblical, and other traditional, depictions of angels.

A Glorious Secret

At the time, the cosmonauts were performing a series of medical experiments aboard the station. They then reported that they had to stop, as a brilliant orange cloud covered the area, blinding them for a moment or two. When they regained their vision, the angels appeared through the cloud. They stayed in the vicinity for 10 or so minutes, but then vanished, and did not reappear again for several days.

However, just over two weeks later, the angels were seen again. This time, the witnesses included Cosmonauts Igor Volk, Vladimir Dzhanibevok, and Svetlana Savitskaya (the second woman to have gone into space, after Valentina Kereshkova,

19 years previously). They later reported that the beings were glowing with a powerful orange light, and that there were seven of the angels: 'They were smiling as though they shared a glorious secret,' the cosmonauts later recalled, 'but within a few minutes, they were gone, and we never saw them again.'

Conspiracy Theory

Subsequent to these reports, a conspiracy theory arose as to the meaning and nature of these angels. According to these theorists, the Hubble Telescope, which was launched into orbit in 1990 and has since been regularly serviced in space by teams of astronauts, has taken pictures of these celestial beings and sent them to earth. In these pictures, the angels are visible, surrounded by the orange glow described by the *Salyut 7* cosmonauts.

These pictures, however – so the conspiracy theory goes – have been suppressed by officials from the Vatican, as well as the US, Soviet and French authorities. This is because the Vatican believes that the pictures would cause a mass panic if they were released. The reason for this is that the 'celestial beings', far from being benign angels bringing good tidings to humanity, are actually harbingers of doom.

The Secret of the Vatican

It is believed that, when the orange cloud was first seen, scientists thought that they had discovered a new cluster of stars. However, when the computer-generated pictures were enlarged, it became clear that the brilliant cloud was, in fact, a group of seven angels flying together through the constellation Carina, which contains Canopus, the second brightest star in the sky, as well as several other very bright clusters of stars. The angels were described thus:

They were about eighty feet tall and had wing spans as large as aeroplanes. Their faces were round and peaceful, and they were all beaming. It seemed like they were overjoyed at being photographed by the Hubble telescope. They seemed to be smiling at each other as if they were letting the rest of the universe in on a glorious secret.

Rumour had it that the Vatican was not best pleased about the pictures, believing the pictures to show the 'the angel of light' warned against in St Paul's *Letter to the Corinthians* in the Bible. Here, St Paul warns against being deceived by false leaders:

'For such are false apostles, deceitful workers, transforming themselves into the apostles of Christ. And no marvel; for Satan himself is transformed into an angel of light. Therefore it is no great thing if his ministers also be transformed as the ministers of righteousness, whose end shall be according to their works.'

According to this interpretation, these angels spelled the coming of Satan and the end of the universe, and thus the Vatican suppressed the release of the pictures. In addition, it is believed that the number seven has a significance here, referring to the seven periods of the church. Currently, we are in the fifth period, which is one of destruction, pain, and suffering. Thus, because broadcasting this information might bring a message of despair to humanity, rather than one of hope, the Vatican has declined to comment on the pictures, or to release them as evidence of the existence of angels.

THE ANGELS OF MONS

At the Battle of Mons in 1914, British soldiers were valiantly fighting off the German opposition when Belgian and French forces were ordered to retreat. Quickly outnumbered, the British were exposed and facing certain defeat. Suddenly, a bright light shone and before the soldiers, ghostly bowmen appeared.

The battle took place on 23 August 1914 and was the first major action of the British Expeditionary Force. The battle was extremely important, not only in military terms, but for the people at home as well, as Britain's performance would boost morale if it were successful. On the battlefield, Belgian and French forces began to retreat, leaving the British behind who became suddenly, and very heavily, outnumbered. They had only one option left, to fight until they could safely withdraw. When the moment came, something extraordinary happened. Out of nowhere, a bright light appeared between the British and German forces, and figures of angels materialized holding crossbows and swords. The angels outstretched their wings forming a protective barrier, allowing the British to escape and stopping the Germans from advancing.

The 'Bowmen'

A legend was born, and back on home soil, a Welsh author named Arthur Machen, wrote a story about the bravery of the British soldiers for a London newspaper, *The Evening News*. Machen was a mystic who was well known for his tales of horror, fantasy, and the supernatural, which included a classic horror story called *The Great God Pan*. On this occasion, Machen decided to fuse his writing as a reporter – he had written several features on the progress of the war for the newspaper – with his talent as a storyteller. The story is set in the time of the retreat from the battle. He told of phantom archers, or 'bowmen' that had appeared to the soldiers. These bowmen, according to the tale, were ghosts of men who had been present at the Battle of Agincourt, a famous 15th-century battle in which the British King, Henry V, himself led his troops into battle and triumphed over a much larger French force. (The battle was also well known because of the superior longbows that the British used).

'Shining Beings'

The story told how, during the battle, British soldiers called upon St George for help, and were amazed to see a row of 'shining beings' armed with longbows, who set about defeating the Germans. It was described in terms of a report from the front, and the newspaper neglected to mention that it was fiction.

The patriotic story hit a nerve, inspiring the British public, and rumours quickly spread that it was true. Machen himself was surprised by the reaction, since he had apparently not realized that the newspaper had printed the story as fact. He later said that he had never intended to create a hoax, and was bewildered at the response. He had several requests from editors of parish magazines to reprint the story, and it began to be regarded as a true report. When he was asked if he would write a short introduction to a pamphlet about the 'occurrence', he declined, and began to realize that he had set off a major deception. He commented:

It seemed that my light fiction had been accepted by the congregation of this particular church as the solidest of facts; and it was then that it began to dawn on me that if I had failed in the art of letters, I had succeeded, unwittingly, in the art of deceit. This happened, I should think, some time in April, and the snowball of rumour that was then

From the painting by W. H. Margetson

"THE ANGELS OF MONS."

A postcard depicting the Angel of Mons, taken from a painting by W. H. Margetson.

set rolling has been rolling ever since, growing bigger and bigger, till it is now swollen to a monstrous size.

Nevertheless, despite Machen's protestations, the legend continued to grow. Eye witnesses told how they had seen dead German soldiers on the field of battle, covered in wounds that could only have been made by arrows.

Angelic Warriors

The story was taken up by psychics, mediums, and an account was published in an influential British spiritualist magazine. This feature told of how a supernatural force came to help the British soldiers in their hour of need. Some described the force as being a host of angelic warriors, others as seeing an unusually bright, luminous cloud above the armies; yet others were convinced that the divine aid came from medieval bowmen led by St George. As in ancient times, stories about the hand of God intervening to help the patriotic cause were rife.

The next episode in this strange story was that by 1915, sermons about the Angels of Mons were becoming popular in churches of all denominations in Britain. The story was told to show how God was on the side of the British, and would help England win the war against the Germans. When Machen tried to cool the situation by republishing the story and explaining that it was fiction, his action only fanned the flames of dissent. The book became a bestseller, and many enthusiasts set about finding evidence for its claims.

HOAX, RUMOUR, OR PROPAGANDA?

The next twist in the story was that a well-respected body called the Society for Psychical Research conducted a serious enquiry into the phenomenon, and concluded that there was no evidence to suggest that a heavenly host of angels, or bowmen, had succeeded in helping the British soldiers keep back the German army on the first day of the battle. The society pointed out that there were no eye witness accounts of what happened, and that the 'visions' alleged to have taken place proved, on investigation, 'to be founded on mere rumour' and could not be 'traced to any authoritative source'. This seemed to be a compelling argument, particularly as it came from a body that actually believed in the existence of supernatural forces and the paranormal.

Some believe that the increasing number of rumours that occurred in 1915 were not simply the work of credulous members of the public. It has been argued that the Angels of Mons story was actually circulated as part of the propaganda machine of the British government, in order to improve morale after a series of crushing defeats. During this period, the British had been unable to push forward on the Western Front, and a large British ship, the Lusitania, had sunk after being torpedoed by the Germans, with the loss of over a thousand lives.

Phantom Cavalrymen

However, some stories that came to light seemed to suggest that something strange had happened at the Battle of Mons, though no one was quite sure what it was. A few named soldiers gave accounts of seeing visions of ghost-like cavalrymen rather than angels or archers. These visions appeared to them during the retreat from the battle, rather than when the British were attacking the German forces. It has been suggested by some commentators that these 'visions' may have been the result of hallucinations caused by illness or wounding, lack of sleep and food, and general mental instability caused by the experience of war.

In retrospect, it seems that the Angels of Mons story demonstrates the importance of religion in wartime situations, and the eagerness on the part of the population to believe that divine providence will favour the combatants on one's own side. It is also an example of how quickly rumours spread in the context of any great social upheaval, especially wartime, when people are panicked and afraid, and seek comfort in familiar religious icons. In addition, the Angels of Mons story provided an important boost to morale in the context of the initial stages of World War I, and as such may have had an element of propaganda to it.

The Legend That Will Not Die

Nevertheless, the story has continued to inspire and fascinate people across the world, and is still remembered to this day. Indeed, in the 1980s, the tale of the Angels of Mons was revived by Christian and New Age movements in the US, where it was published in several books and magazines. More recently, in 2001, the British newspaper *The Sunday Times* ran an article about the Angels of Mons, claiming that a veteran World War I soldier, William Doidge, had photographic and film evidence of the phenomenon, and that an angel had also been seen in Woodchester Mansion, a large country house in the English Cotswolds that was mysteriously abandoned in 1873.

The footage of the angels, it was alleged, had been found in a trunk in an antique shop in Caerleon, close to where Arthur Machen had once lived. Marlon Brando, so the article related, had put up a large sum of money for it, and was planning to use it to make a major motion picture about the Angels of Mons. This story was later found to be a complete hoax, and became the subject of a BBC radio documentary entitled, *The Making of an Urban Myth*.

What remains extraordinary in this tale, however, is how quickly the legend of the Angels of Mons spread during World War I, so much so that it became almost treasonable, at the time, to doubt it. For many years afterwards, commentators continued to believe it, despite Machen's insistence that the story was fiction, which he supported by the lack of a reliable first-hand witness at the battle. Even the well respected historian, A.J. P. Taylor, noted in his history of the war published in 1963, that the battle was the only one in which 'supernatural intervention was observed, more or less reliably, on the British side.' And today, periodically, the legend of the Angels of Mons, who came to the aid of the British in their hour of need, continues to be revived.

The Angels of Mons, c.20th century.

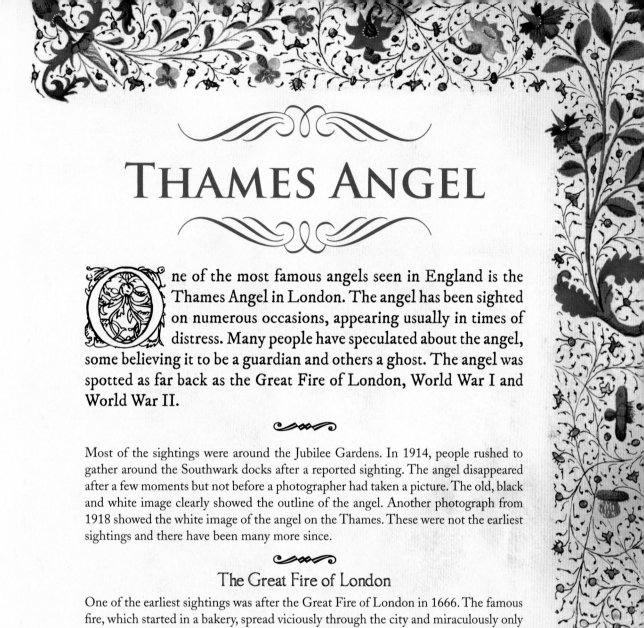

THAMES ANGEL

One of the most famous angels seen in England is the Thames Angel in London. The angel has been sighted on numerous occasions, appearing usually in times of distress. Many people have speculated about the angel, some believing it to be a guardian and others a ghost. The angel was spotted as far back as the Great Fire of London, World War I and World War II.

Most of the sightings were around the Jubilee Gardens. In 1914, people rushed to gather around the Southwark docks after a reported sighting. The angel disappeared after a few moments but not before a photographer had taken a picture. The old, black and white image clearly showed the outline of the angel. Another photograph from 1918 showed the white image of the angel on the Thames. These were not the earliest sightings and there have been many more since.

The Great Fire of London

One of the earliest sightings was after the Great Fire of London in 1666. The famous fire, which started in a bakery, spread viciously through the city and miraculously only killed six people. Workers, who were busy rebuilding the city after three quarters had burnt down, spotted the 'holy apparition', believing it to be an angel. Six sightings were documented in total including that of Samuel Pepys who logged his sighting in his diary. People were calmed by the sightings, some believing the angel to be watching over them. They believed that the angel appearing six times was connected to the six men who died in the fire. The sightings after the deaths from the fire seemed to appear in sixes, prompting people to believe that the apparition may not be an angel but the six souls lost in the fire. The people of the city were brought closer together as they united to help those in need. The appearance of the angel was thought of as a sign,

showing the people hope and guidance through a difficult time. At the time, the angel was referred to as the 'angel of promise', appearing in times of difficulty as a sign of good times to come. Those who noted the sightings stated that they were not afraid of the apparition, but felt calm and at ease. It was the Great Fire of London that is thought to have cleared the city of the plague, a disease that was rapidly wiping out the English population at the time. This cleansing of the city was linked to the angelic figure. People have thought that perhaps it was not the fire that removed the plague but the angel.

Recent Sightings

The angel sightings did not end with the six immediately after the Great Fire of London. There have been another four since. Some believers think that there will be another two sightings to complete the pattern of six sightings. Some people are fearful as the sightings have previously come after times of peril and distress. If the pattern is correct, suffering may possibly come in the future. Nowadays, technology has advanced and sightings of the Thames Angel have been caught on camera. In 2006, British presenter David Grant was filming for a new television talent show on the Thames banks. He was caught on camera becoming suddenly distracted by something hovering over the Thames – he had seen the angel. His expression showed shock over seeing such a sight and he mumbled what he had seen to the cameraman.

Another noted sighting in 2006 was that of Jemima Waterhouse, a student at the University of Greenwich. Jemima was walking to meet a friend when she saw a winged apparition hovering over the Thames. At first, she was so shocked that she could not absorb what she was seeing. After a few seconds, she took a photo on her camera phone but the image showed up blurry. Her friend then joined her but when she tried to see what Waterhouse was looking at she saw nothing. The apparition had disappeared. It was not just the sighting that amazed Waterhouse but how she felt afterwards.

'I felt a sense of calm spreading over me. It was comforting and familiar, a kind of peace that lasted for a while after. It's really hard to put into words but I guess you could describe it as peace of mind.'

When Jemima and her friend got home, they went to look at the picture on the computer to see if the quality would improve. They saw a distinct outline of what could only be described as a winged figure. Other friends thought the image was a trick but Waterhouse knew what she had seen. She found an unexpected believer in Dr Miriam Hayles who worked at her University. She read Waterhouse's essay on the apparition and became interested in her story. Hayles informed Waterhouse about the Thames angel sightings and then took her to the library to show her similar stories in the history books. Waterhouse was shocked but knew that she was blessed to have seen such a vision.

Around the same time, there was another spotting which was also captured on camera.

Mario Daniello, who had come out of Waterloo train station stopped to have a picture taken by the Thames. He stated that he suddenly felt full of laughter and happiness, a common feeling between the witnesses. The image in his photo showed a blurry winged, white figure behind him. He did not see the angel directly but he felt that something spiritual was there.

Theories

There have been many theories about the Thames Angel. Some believe that there are people who have certain abilities that allow them to see the angel when others cannot. Others believe the angel not to be a messenger from God but a pure spirit who guards the city. There are some people who believe in the ancient angel of promise; this particular theory compares the Thames Angel to the rainbow of promise in Genesis. The idea was that the sighting of the angel was a promise from God that whatever disaster that had occurred would not happen again. However, the recent sightings test that theory as there were no disasters that happened. One thing that all of the different theories have in common is that none dispute the angel being good; all of the sightings noted that the angel radiated calm and tranquility. The angel has been seen in photographs, CCTV, video and by the naked eye and it has been the inspiration for many artists who have tried to capture the mysterious figure in paintings and drawings. It is evident that the angel has many recorded sightings throughout history and remains still active in making appearances on the Thames. The angel gives feelings of hope and serenity to those who see it. The idea that a spiritual being has been protecting the city and watching over its people is one that the people of London find very comforting and uplifting.

ANTONIA D'ASTONAC AND THE ARCHANGEL MICHAEL

In the 18th century, in the year 1751, a Carmelite nun, Antonia d'Astonac, reported an encounter with the archangel Michael. She reported that he appeared to her one day and told her that he wished to be honoured by nine salutations corresponding to the nine choirs of angels.

'By the intercession of St. Michael and the celestial choir of seraphim, may the Lord make us worthy to burn with the fire of perfect charity. Amen.'

This and the other salutations were, according to Antonia, to be followed by the recitation of one Our Father prayer and three Hail Mary prayers. The archangel continued:

'Whoever practices this devotion will have an escort of nine angels when approaching the altar to receive communion, will have my continuous assistance and that of all the angels throughout life, and will have deliverance from purgatory for himself and his relatives after death.'

St Michael's Chaplet

The archangel also ordered the reciting of a chaplet, or prayer, in his honour. It cites all the types of angels that are mentioned in the Bible:

1. By the intercession of Michael, the Archangel and the celestial Choir of Seraphim, may the Lord make us worthy to burn with the fire of perfect charity. Amen.

2. By the intercession of Michael, the Archangel and the celestial Choir of Cherubim, may the Lord grant us the grace to leave the ways of sin and run in the paths of Christian perfection. Amen.

3. By the intercession of Michael, the Archangel and the celestial Choir of Thrones, may the Lord infuse into our hearts a true and sincere spirit of humility. Amen.

4. By the intercession of Michael, the Archangel and the celestial Choir of Dominions, may the Lord give us grace to govern our senses and overcome any unruly passions. Amen.

5. By the intercession of Michael, the Archangel and the celestial Choir of Powers, may the Lord protect our souls against the snares and temptations of the devil. Amen.

6. By the intercession of Michael, the Archangel and the celestial Choir of Virtues, may the Lord preserve us from evil and falling into temptation. Amen.

7. By the intercession of Michael, the Archangel and the celestial Choir of Principalities, may God fill our souls with a true spirit of obedience. Amen.

8. By the intercession of Michael, the Archangel and the celestial Choir of Archangels, may the Lord give us perseverance in faith and in all good works in order that we may attain the glory of Heaven. Amen.

9. By the intercession of Michael, the Archangel and the celestial Choir of Angels, may the Lord grant us to be protected by them in this mortal life and conducted in the life to come to Heaven. Amen.

The supplicant was then instructed to say prayers in honour of the archangels Gabriel, Raphael and his or her Guardian Angel. A further prayer was then required:

O Glorious Prince Michael, the Archangel, Chief and Commander of the Heavenly Hosts, Guardian of Souls, Vanquisher of Rebel Spirits, Servant in the House of the Divine King and our Admirable Conductor, you who shine with excellence and superhuman virtue deliver us from all evil, who turn to you with confidence and enable us by your gracious protection to serve God more and more faithfully every day. Pray for us, O Glorious Michael, the Archangel, Prince of the Church of Jesus Christ, that we may be made worthy of His Promises. Almighty and Everlasting God, who, by a prodigy of goodness and merciful desire for the salvation of all men, has appointed the most glorious Archangel Michael, the Archangel, Prince of Your Church, make us worthy, we ask You, to be delivered from all our enemies, that none of them may harass us at the hour of death, but that we may be conducted by him into Your Presence. This we ask through the merits of Jesus Christ Our Lord. Amen.

In 1851, Pope Pius IX approved this chaplet, and it became part of the liturgy of the Catholic church. In this way, Antonia d'Astonac's vision of the Archangel Michael, and her prayer to the angel, was incorporated into Catholic doctrine, and remains an important aspect of angelology in the Catholic church to this day.

THE VISION OF JOSEPH SMITH JR

Joseph Smith Jr was a 19th-century American religious leader, who believed that an angel had appeared to him in a vision and told him about a book of golden plates containing a history of early American peoples, which were buried in a box near to Smith's home. Smith retrieved the plates, which were apparently inscribed with this story, and reported that he had been able to translate the unknown language written on the plates into English.

In 1830, he published his translation of the golden plates as the *Book of Mormon*. He attracted many followers, and established what later became known as the Church of the Latter Day Saints. Smith also gave an account of his vision, which he described in the following terms:

While I was thus in the act of calling upon God, I discovered a light appearing in my room, which continued to increase until the room was lighter than at noonday, when immediately a personage appeared at my bedside, standing in the air, for his feet did not touch the floor. He had on a loose robe of most exquisite whiteness. It was a whiteness beyond anything earthly I had ever seen; nor do I believe that any earthly thing could be made to appear so exceedingly white and brilliant....Not only was his robe exceedingly white, but his whole person was glorious beyond description, and his countenance truly like lightning. The room was exceedingly light, but not so very bright as immediately around his person. When I first looked upon him, I was afraid; but the fear soon left me.

The Angel Moroni

Smith later identified the angel as the Angel Moroni, who continued to visit him after his first vision on 21 September 1823. The angel also appeared to other witnesses. The angel was said to be a reincarnation of an ancient prophet and warrior who had died fighting a battle between two pre-Columbian civilizations. The prophet was resurrected as an angel, and entrusted with the golden plates of the *Book of Mormon*, which he then gave to Joseph Smith Jr, who went on to found his own church.

There is some confusion in certain quarters as to the real nature of the Angel Moroni. Some have pointed to the fact that in early descriptions of the angel, Smith referred to him as 'Nephi', who is mentioned in the *Book of Mormon* as the author of the first two volumes and the leader of the Nephite people, who lived around 600 bc. The name was later changed to Moroni. Others claim that Moroni could well be a manifestation of Lucifer, or one of the fallen angels. This is based on an observation by St Paul in his *Letter to the Corinthians* that Satan sometimes masquerades as 'an angel of light'. However, since most angels are described as being surrounded by bright light, this does not seem to be a very specific objection. A few critics have mentioned the fact that the name 'Moroni' occurs in the adventure stories of Captain William Kidd, with which Smith may have been familiar. Kidd was thought to have buried his treasure in the Comoros Islands, whose capital city is Moroni. The theory goes

that Smith also got the idea of 'buried treasure' – the golden plates – from the Kidd stories, and named the hill where he found the plates 'Cumorah', which is a rather similar name to Comoros. However, this is simply conjecture, as the apologists for the Church of the Latter Day Saints point out. In modern day images of the Angel Moroni, such as statues, he is often shown blowing a trumpet and standing on the cover of the *Book of Mormon*.

MORTAL ANGELS

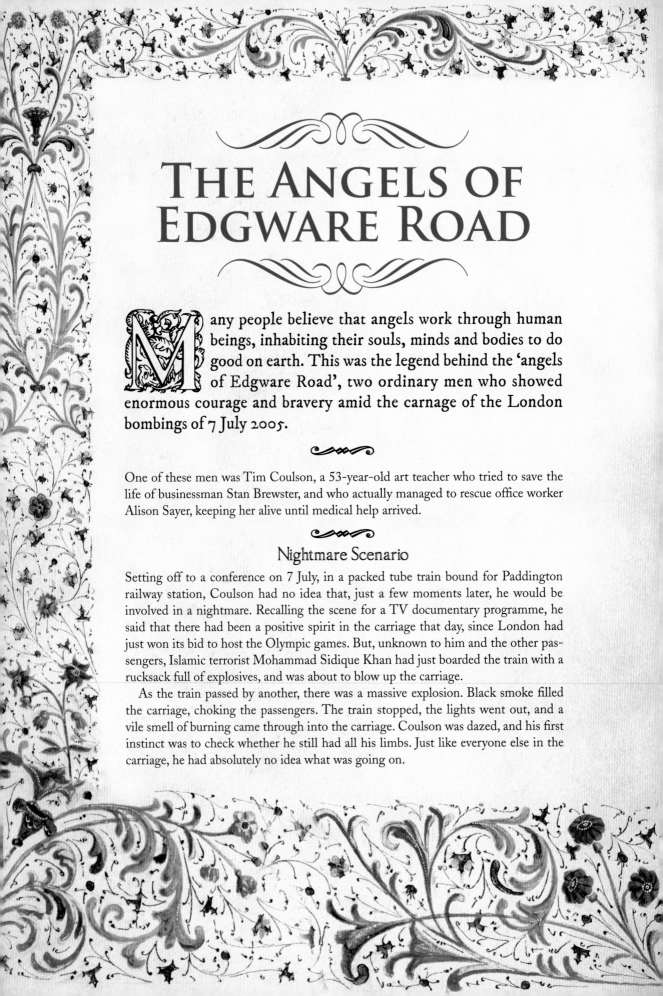

THE ANGELS OF EDGWARE ROAD

Many people believe that angels work through human beings, inhabiting their souls, minds and bodies to do good on earth. This was the legend behind the 'angels of Edgware Road', two ordinary men who showed enormous courage and bravery amid the carnage of the London bombings of 7 July 2005.

One of these men was Tim Coulson, a 53-year-old art teacher who tried to save the life of businessman Stan Brewster, and who actually managed to rescue office worker Alison Sayer, keeping her alive until medical help arrived.

Nightmare Scenario

Setting off to a conference on 7 July, in a packed tube train bound for Paddington railway station, Coulson had no idea that, just a few moments later, he would be involved in a nightmare. Recalling the scene for a TV documentary programme, he said that there had been a positive spirit in the carriage that day, since London had just won its bid to host the Olympic games. But, unknown to him and the other passengers, Islamic terrorist Mohammad Sidique Khan had just boarded the train with a rucksack full of explosives, and was about to blow up the carriage.

As the train passed by another, there was a massive explosion. Black smoke filled the carriage, choking the passengers. The train stopped, the lights went out, and a vile smell of burning came through into the carriage. Coulson was dazed, and his first instinct was to check whether he still had all his limbs. Just like everyone else in the carriage, he had absolutely no idea what was going on.

Horrific Injuries

Then a message came over the public address system, asking people with first-aid and medical skills to go to the back of the train. Although Tim did not have any specialist training, instead of rushing away from the scene as quickly as possible, like most of the other passengers, an instinct told him to stay and help those who had been injured. This was despite the fact that it was a dangerous, frightening scene, and that many of the wounded had horrific injuries. Out of the hundreds of passengers on the train, there were only two others who stayed, like him, to see if they could give assistance: Canadian writer Peter Zimonjic and arts graduate Susanna Pell.

The three 'angels' found an emergency toolbar and shattered the glass window of the carriage. Inside, they found a bloodbath. It was still dark, and most of the surviving passengers were unable to hear when they called out to them, because their eardrums had been perforated by the blast. Nevertheless, the 'angels' went in to see what they could do to help. Coulson picked his way past the bodies to a man whose upper body was coming out of a hole in the floor of the train. He was alive, but unable to move. To free the man's legs, Coulson crawled underneath the train, but to his horror found that the legs were lying on the ground below, separated from the man's body. He went back up, and cradled the man in his arms until he died. When the man was dead, Coulson said a prayer over him, and closed his eyes for him.

Coulson later discovered that the man was Michael Brewster, known as 'Stan', and that he was the same age as himself. Brewster had been travelling into London for a conference, like him. Coulson remembers feeling sad when he realized that the parallels between victim and rescuer were so close; it could easily have been he, not Brewster, who died in the train that day.

Saving a Life

Having been through this trauma, Coulson then went on to find another injured person to help. He responded to the screams of a young woman lying on the track, who had been thrown from the train. Alison Sayer had been knocked unconscious by the blow, and was just coming round, confused and frightened. She was also badly injured, losing blood from a wounded leg, and with a swollen eye. Coulson was aware that she might die, but he did not convey his fears to her; instead, he kept her talking, trying to distract her so that she would not panic. All the while, he was worrying about what had happened, and whether more explosions were on the way. He was also worried about staying because he had a wife and three grown-up children and felt a responsibility to get out of harm's way for their sake. However, he did not communicate his fears to the young woman, and remained with her, talking her through her pain and terror.

After a gruelling hour, Coulson saw a light coming down the tunnel. It was a paramedic carrying a torch. He helped the paramedic administer oxygen to the injured woman, and accompanied the pair of them up into the station, holding the oxygen cylinder. When he saw the sunlight of the street, he felt numb. He later said, 'I don't remember feeling relief. I don't remember feeling anything.'

Post-Traumatic Stress

At the hospital, Coulson was able to contact his wife, and went home. However, after the event he suffered from post-traumatic stress, which continued for months. Alison Sayer was operated on at the hospital, and doctors managed to save both her leg and her sight. She then went home to Australia, where she and Coulson began a close correspondence. Later that year, Coulson was given an award from the Royal Humane Society, and Sayer sent an open letter telling the world about his bravery.

Coulson managed to recover from the horror of his experience by going for a walk every day by the river Thames, and by looking out at his garden full of roses, tended by his wife. However, after the incident, he was unable to resume his work, having continued to experience post-traumatic stress. Although he underwent cognitive behaviour therapy and tried to go back to teaching, he found himself unable to do so.

Today, he is sad about the lost opportunity to teach, which was a job that he loved, but bears no resentment about what happened to him. He reasons that since the bomber is dead – he saw his body at the scene – there is no point in feeling angry about the events. However, he does find it hard to believe that anyone would willingly cause such suffering to innocent people. He remains philosophical about the deep mental scars he has been left with, which he knows will never completely heal. 'I have come to accept that I won't be the person I was,' he says, 'but that's fine with me.'

Happy Ending

Another unlikely 'angel' at the scene was an ex-firefighter, Paul Dadge, who was walking up Edgware Road when he came across the scene of chaos following the bomb explosion. Instead of hurrying away, he stayed to help set up an emergency medical centre at a nearby store, Marks and Spencers, dealing with the walking wounded. During this process, which involved coordinating and comforting hundreds of frightened, injured people, there was an emergency alert, and the store was evacuated. He went outside with a patient, Davinia Turrell, who was wearing a mask over her burned face. As they walked out, Dadge heard the click of a hundred cameras, and knew that their picture would be in the papers the next day.

His prediction proved right, and the next day, the image had been sent around the world: the striking image of the woman in the mask with Dadge beside her. Dadge and Turrell were offered money for their stories, but Turrell did not want to talk to the press. Dadge did talk eventually, though he insists that he did not receive payment for the interviews. He said that the bombing had changed his perception of Londoners as selfish and thoughtless, and that he had realized there was a spirit of community among people when disaster struck. He also announced that, when the pictures hit the papers, an old girlfriend got in touch with him. The pair were reunited, and have been together ever since.

Edgware Road train station, London, the morning of the terrorist attacks of 7/7/2005.

TSUNAMI ANGELS

On 6 December 2004, an undersea earthquake caused a series of catastrophic tsunamis across the coasts of the Indian Ocean. Waves up to 100ft tall crashed into 14 countries, killing over 230,000 people. Thailand, Indonesia, India and Sri Lanka were hit the hardest and suffered severe damage. The earthquake that caused the natural disaster was the third largest to ever be recorded.

TILLY SMITH

In 2004, the Tilly Smith and family from Surrey, England, were on Mai Khao beach, Thailand on holiday. They were enjoying a day out when 11-year-old Tilly noticed that the sea had gone frothy and was bubbling. She recognized these signs of an imminent tsunami as she had learnt about the Hawaii tsunami in a school geography lesson two weeks prior. Tilly sought out her parents immediately. She told them what she had seen but they were unconvinced. She became inpatient with her parents' disbelief and grew hysterical; she knew that a tsunami was about to hit but no one believed her. Her instincts told her to get as far away from the coast as possible but did not want to leave her family and the people on the beach behind. After Smith pleaded with her parents, her father went and told a security guard about his daughter's prediction. The guard raised the alarms and more than 100 people were immediately evacuated from the beach. After the evacuation, the tsunami hit the shore as predicted by the young girl. Because of this prediction, Mai Khao beach was one of the only beaches on the island to have no reported casualties.

Tilly, who had saved over 100 people, was regarded as an angel who had foreseen a devastating event. She was the only person to predict the tsunami on Mai Khao beach. People were intrigued as to why only a child saw the signs of the disaster, some theo-

rizing that it was because she was destined to save all those people – the act of an angel. Because of Smith's courage and determination, she received the Thomas Gray Special Award by the Marine Society and Sea Cadets. She also appeared at the United Nations a year after the tsunami hit and met with the American president. Smith attended in order to highlight the importance of education but others believe her prediction not to be an educated guess but an act of fate. Tilly Smith will forever be thought of as an angel in Thailand.

JESS MAULDER

Jess Maulder, a medical student from Melbourne, Australia, was in Thailand on holiday in 2004. When the tsunami struck, there was devastation and death everywhere. Maulder instinctively knew she wanted to help so she became a volunteer, working in a morgue 250km south of Phuket. She worked diligently, initially helping doctors identify dead bodies in the morgue. One of her roles was to lay out the dead bodies and note unique features that could help to identify the deceased. It was a difficult job but Maulder was courageous and showed professionalism and composure. She was one of the few international volunteers to initially assist after the tsunami.

After leaving Thailand, Maulder spent the remainder of her university break aiding victims of the tsunami in Sri Lanka. She situated herself at Arugam Bay a centre of the devastation. When the tsunami hit, over 200 people were killed there as the 12m waves came crashing 2km inland. Thousands of people lost their homes as most of the buildings were brought crashing down by the monstrous waves. With help from her brother, Maulder got to work. She was shocked and appalled that the abandoned people affected had not yet received government aid or attention from relief organizations. The pair helped build homes, shops and roads but most of their work

went into helping those at refugee camps. Many diseases circulated quickly due to the dirty, damp conditions. There were few doctors so Maulder had to treat many of the injured herself, with little medical supplies. She not only treated the injured and sick, but also gave comfort and sympathy to those who had lost loved ones. Maulder spent countless hours trying to identify dead bodies and lost people. She wanted to reunite the dead with their families so that the families would have peace of mind. Her charity and tenderness lead people to believe that she is a modern day angel and tsunami hero.

'I think when I get home it will be difficult for people to understand the magnitude of suffering we have seen. They don't see the families who have to come to collect the totally monstrous bodies left.'

In recognition of her efforts, Maulder was voted Australian Woman of the Year by Age readers. Maulder wished to return to Phuket on the anniversary of the tsunami to attend the memorial service but the Australian government refused to fund her. The government stated that they only fund those who had lost loved ones to attend the service, not volunteers. However, Australian travel agent David Goldman recognized Maulder's efforts during the tsunami and reserved her complimentary flights so that she could attend. Maulder did not have a duty to help; she helped out of kindness and love. She had comforted many bereaved people and was a valuable volunteer in the most devastated places. Maulder and Smith, who were both holiday-makers, did everything in their power to save lives and make a difference. They will always be remembered as tsunami angels.

Tilly Smith, 'Angel of the Beach', reads poetry during a ceremony to commemorate the victims of the 2005 tsnunami in Thailand.

THE ANGELS OF 9/11

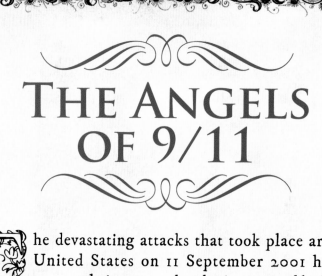

The devastating attacks that took place around the United States on 11 September 2001 have been constantly interpreted and reinterpreted by historians and social commentators since that fateful day when nearly 3,000 victims, including the 19 hijackers, lost their lives. In New York, 343 firefighters and 60 police officers also perished as they attended the scene; they are sometimes referred to as, 'the angels of 9/11'.

In an attempt to make sense of the atrocity, many people have read religious significance into the events, claiming that angels were present – whether in the shape of the brave rescuers, or in the form of the 'falling angels' that jumped out of skyscrapers to their deaths. The language of religious morality, of good and evil, angels and devils, has also been reinforced by American government leaders, such as President Bush, and by a deeply religious population shocked and horrified at the brutality of the attack on the heart of the nation.

Satan in the Smoke

One of the most common of these religious theories is that the face of the angel of death, or Satan, could be seen in the smoke pouring out of the Twin Towers. According to this account, a quote from the *Book of Revelation* (significantly, chapter 9:11) reads:

'And they had a king over them, which is the angle of the bottomless pit, whose name in the Hebrew tongue is Abbadon (Destruction), but in the Greek tongue hath his name Apollyon (Destroyer).'

Footage of the disaster has since been analyzed by various experts, and at certain points you can see imagery form in the plumes of smoke. One frame reveals a pattern of skeletal heads, and in one instance, a skeletal figure with its arm outstretched, waving what seems to be a weapon. Forms of wings in the smoke can also been seen, outlined against the sky. No one can deny that the scene of attack on the World Trade Center was certainly like a biblical vision of hell, with fire, smoke, ash, wreckage, and panic-stricken human beings trapped below the burning towers.

The 'Axis of Evil'

The idea of 'evil' having visited America on that day was taken up by President Bush directly after the events of 9/11. Rather than pinpointing the culprits as a small band of crazed religious fanatics, he declared a nationwide War on Terror, and in an address to the nation, spoke of an 'axis of evil' that America must fight against in order to preserve decency and democracy throughout the world. His choice of words revealed that he, along with many other Americans, was still a fervent believer in a deeply religious, Old Testament. An ideology that had changed little since the 19th century, in which the world was pictured as a place of avenging angels, evil spirits, and an ongoing conflict between the forces of good and evil, still being waged daily in the new millennium. It is perhaps partly for this reason that the smoke plumes of the burning Twin Towers continue to be analyzed for sightings of the 'angel of death' visiting horror and destruction on an innocent population, out of a tranquil, clear blue sky on that sunny morning in September 2001.

The 'Falling Angel'

In addition to the 'angel of death' theory, much speculation surrounds a photograph of an unknown falling man jumping out of one of the towers to avoid being burned alive or choking to death in the fumes. The shot, taken by photographer Richard Drew at 9:41 am, as the chaos grew more terrifying, shows a man falling down the side of the skyscraper, upside down. He appears to be falling headfirst – though in fact, as it has been pointed out, this photo was only a still, and other shots in the same sequence show him tumbling down to the ground in the normal way.

Despite many attempts to find out exactly who the man was, his identity remains a mystery, and thus today, he continues to stands as a symbol of the events of 9/11, just as the tomb of the Unknown Soldier reminds us of the great wars fought by forgotten soldiers during the course of history.

A Symbol of Our Time?

However, unlike the Unknown Soldier, the Falling Angel, as he has been called, is very much an image of our time: he is not fighting a war on a battlefield, or even in an aeroplane, but heading down to his death alone, flying through the air, having jumped in panic from a high window in a New York skyscraper, one of the great symbols of modern capitalism. We are aware, when we look at the photograph, that the man has panicked, and jumped on impulse: he does not know what caused the explosion, or why it has happened. His enemy is unseen, and unknown. His death comes suddenly, and he has no control, power, or understanding of his fate. His abrupt, unexpected descent towards death on a routine day when he went to work in his office is perhaps what the 21st century humanity fears most: the sudden wiping out of our increasingly complex global civilization, whether through 'evil' or unforeseen natural disaster, causing instant death, so that we cannot review our lives, plan for the living, or even say goodbye to our loved ones.

In this context, it is easy to see why President Bush would have called up an ancient belief system, focusing on the war between good and evil, to try to explain what happened on 9/11. He may have felt that the simple Christian message of fighting evil with good, of upholding decency against an onslaught of brutality, was a clear, comforting antidote to the panic-inducing alienation of modern life, in which we all know that disasters – whether terrorist attacks or other major problems caused by the malfunctioning of our increasingly technical world – can come out of the blue. He may also have been trying to reassure the population that its political masters were in control, and were able to protect them from attack, despite the fact that, quite clearly, on that fateful day, they were not. Thus, for many, the image of the 'falling angel' has become iconic, and seems to sum up our fear that 21st century man is lost, alienated, powerless and alone, as if suspended in space, heading abruptly towards destruction.

There has been much speculation on the events on 9/11, but one fact that cannot be disputed is the heroism displayed by New York's various emergency response units. In addition to these brave men and women, many of whom lost colleagues that day, there have been reports of mysterious helpers at the scene. One woman claimed that she was led out of the rubble and dust of the collapsed South Tower by a figure, one that she cannot accurately describe now, and that when she found herself outside and free from danger, this figure had disappeared. A man who was working in the North Tower described how he was trapped beneath some concrete and waiting anxiously for help to arrive. He prayed to himself that the emergency services would find him, and as he started to fear the worst, a sense of calm fell over him, and he felt as if his body was aglow with hope and peace. Seconds later, firefighters found him and saved his life. There are many who believe angels attended the scene that day, of the mortal and immortal kind.

Angel in the smoke. A sole survivor surveys the devastation of 9/11.

FLORENCE NIGHTINGALE

lorence Nightingale was born on 12 May 1820 in Florence, Italy. Her mother Frances Smith and father William Edward Nightingale were a wealthy couple who toured Europe for the first two years of their marriage. When Florence was 17 she had a calling from God to help others but was unsure about how to do it. She decided to turn to nursing.

Ministering Angel

In 1850, Florence began her nursing training at the Institute of St Vincent de Paul in Alexandria, Egypt. On her return to London, she took unpaid work at the Establishment for Gentlewomen During Illness on Harley Street.

When the Crimean war began, Florence, in response to a letter from her friend Sidney Herbert, travelled to Turkey to oversee the nurses in military hospitals. Florence was disturbed by the hospital system and set out for change. She fought for better conditions within the hospital and as a result reduced the mortality rate dramatically. On her return to London, Florence proceeded to fight for basic improvements in military hospitals in England and in doing so gained attention from Queen Victoria. Florence's case was heard and from this the establishment of the Royal Commission on the Health of the Army was born. Due to her spirited achievements, Florence became the first woman to be elected a member of the Royal Statistical Society. It was during this time that a report in *The Times* talked about Florence as an angel, an idea which demonstrates how she was perceived at the time.

She is a 'ministering angel' without any exaggeration in these hospitals, and as her slender form glides quietly along each corridor, every poor fellow's face softens with gratitude at the sight of her. When all the medical officers have retired for the night and silence and darkness have settled down upon those miles of prostrate sick, she may be observed alone, with a little lamp in her hand, making her solitary rounds.

Florence then established the Nightingale Training School for Nurses at St Thomas' Hospital in London. The Nightingale model was used to train nurses and then they were sent all over Britain. They used the model to ensure that British military hospitals were sanitary and efficient. Her *Notes on Nursing* was published and her theories are still used today.

A Selfless Life

Florence had a clear regard for others and helped save many people. She was regarded as a saint for her righteous, selfless ways, but was a humble woman who was uncomfortable in the public spotlight. She dedicated her life to helping and saving lives, living a life of self-sacrifice so she could answer a greater calling. Some thought of her as an angel sent to help people. It is clear that she was a guardian with tender sympathies for the needy. In 1883, Queen Victoria awarded Florence the Royal Red Cross for her work and in 1907 she became the first woman to achieve the Order of Merit from Edward VII. Florence died in 1910 unmarried. Her choice not to marry was not due to a lack of opportunity. She believed that God had marked her to be a single woman and to fulfil her destiny as an earthly angel.

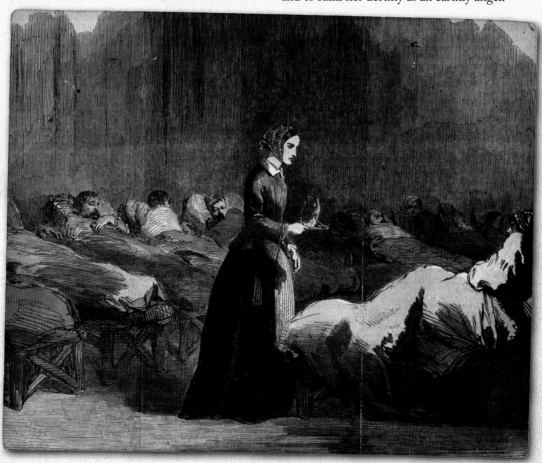

Florence Nightingale, the Lady of the Lamp, tending wounded soldiers.

MARY JANE SEACOLE

Mary Jane Seacole was born Mary Grant in Kingston, Jamaica, in 1805. Her father was a Scottish military officer and her mother a Jamaican descendant of African slaves. Mary's mother was a kind and giving woman who kept a boarding house for recuperating soldiers. Mary was mixed race and because of racial inequality at the time her family had few rights. But Mary was determined to make a change.

Mother Seacole

Mary became educated and skilled in nursing. When the Crimean war broke out she travelled to England to ask the War Office to send her out to tend to injured soldiers. The War Office denied her request. The refusal only fuelled Mary's desire to help so she funded her own way to Crimea where in 1856, she established the British Hotel where she worked to create safe and comfortable quarters for wounded and sick soldiers. This she funded alone. Having previously spent time in the Caribbean, Central America and Britain, Mary learnt European medical ideas, which she then combined with her own traditional methods. Mary was charitable, selfless and was known to visit the battlefield even under fire to tend to wounded soldiers. Her bravery and kindness got her known as 'Mother Seacole'. This was also because she treated the soldiers as dearly as if they were her sons. However, after the war ended Mary became bankrupt as all her money had gone into the hotel – although money was insignificant to her as she felt that helping others was priceless. The British press did not feel the same and raised enough money to pay off her debts.

Angel of Mercy

In 1850, Mary travelled to Panama and opened another boarding house as she was disgusted by the insanitary conditions there. Mary saw that tropical diseases were spreading fast, especially cholera. Being a black woman, the locals were reluctant to accept her help initially but Mary prevailed and won their approval. She worked night and day to improve the conditions for patients and in doing so saved many lives and brought about change. Locals then named her 'Angel of Mercy'. She travelled to Jamaica in 1853 just as a severe yellow fever epidemic broke out, yet again she worked diligently to treat the ill.

Mary returned home to England in ill health after spending many years aiding others. In 1857, she published her memoirs *The Wonderful Adventures of Mrs Seacole in Many Lands*. She became a well known figure but her greatest accomplishments lay in her work as a nurse. Mary was a born healer and spent her life battling prejudice in order to make a difference.

Mary Jane Seacole is an unforgettable figure who has touched the hearts of many. She was awarded the Crimean medal, the French Legion of Honour and Turkish Medal for her work. Mary died in 1881 but her legacy still remains. Mary's heavenly work invites us to see her as an earthly angel.

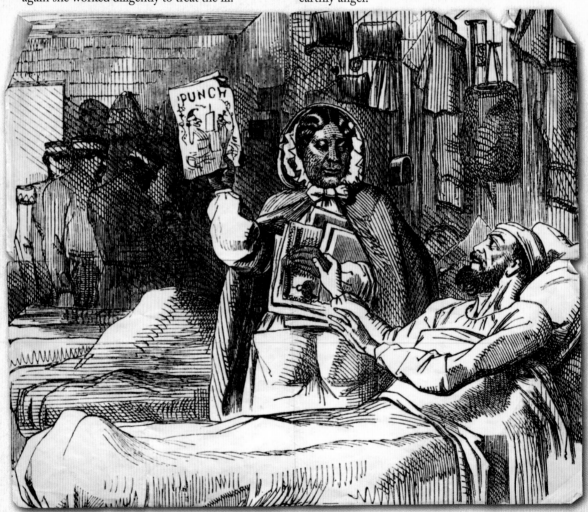

An illustration from an 1857 publication depicting Mary Jane Seacole with a patient.

ANITA GOULDEN

Anita Goulden was born in Manchester, England, in 1919. After a short marriage to John Goulden she decided to take a short holiday to see her brother in Peru. When she arrived she was shocked. She had wanted to see Piura for its beauty. However, it was something else entirely that caught her attention.

Goulden saw many abandoned children collapsed by the roadside, hungry and sick. Most of them were suffering from meningitis or tuberculosis. No one stopped to help or showed any compassion towards the discarded children. Goulden could not believe what she saw and knew that she had to help in any way that she could.

'In all my wildest dreams, I had never thought of human beings in such shocking conditions. The appalling poverty. The indifference of those around.'

In 1957, Goulden decided that she would stay in Piura to help the abandoned children. She used the money that she earned teaching English to assist sick and handicapped children. Her only motive was to help improve the lives of the destitute children. She figured that if no one else was going to help she would do what she could alone. Goulden soon made friends with Anita Mollet, a woman who was travelling home to Piura to work as a volunteer in a children's hospital. Their friendship blossomed and Goulden went to live and work alongside Mollet for many years.

Angel of Piura

In 1982, Goulden decided to move so she could live with the disabled children that she was looking after. She was a determined woman and always strove to bring about change and improve conditions. One child that she aided was called Fedi. She was a young blind girl that Goulden had taken in. Goulden believed in rights

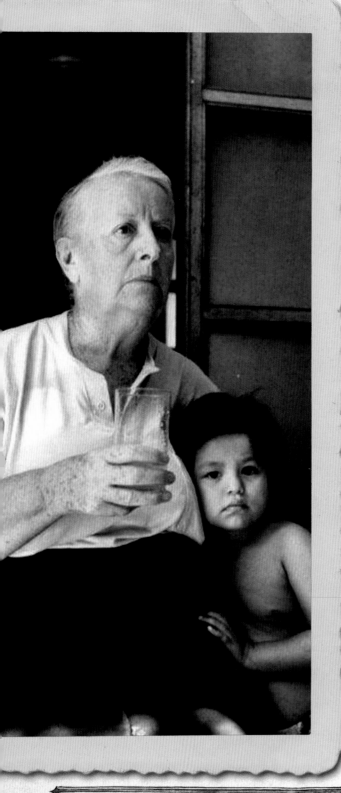

to education for all children no matter if they were healthy or disabled. Fedi wished to study teaching but was refused by her chosen school because of her disability. This angered Goulden who then sought out President Belaunde by climbing through one of his presidential palace windows. She found the president and expressed her thoughts to him regarding Fedi's refusal of education. Within two weeks, Goulden received word that the teaching school Fedi wished to go to would now accept her.

News spread through the villages and towns of this remarkable woman and many poor and disabled children came to Goulden for help. Her home was soon housing around 20 children. The house was small and Goulden struggled with space but could not afford any larger accommodation. She would travel around Peru to seek aid and would often take supplies with her for the hungry, sick and homeless. The Peruvian people named her 'Angel of Piura'.

A True Inspiration

Goulden's hospice grew and she soon found that she was broke and could not afford to fund the operations or even feed the children. Goulden's story back in England brought in funding rapidly and the charity thrived. By the time Goulden died in 2002, she was running a hospice for handicapped children and also a school with over 200 pupils. The Anita Goulden Trust still funds the care of orphaned, abandoned, abused and disabled children in Piura.

Rosemery, a sufferer of spina bifida, knew Goulden when she was nine years old. She benefited strongly from the Anita Goulden Trust, and once told a journalist reporting for UK newspaper *The Telegraph*:

'The first time I saw Anita, I knew she was an angel come down from heaven.'

Anita Goulden, an angel from heaven.

DR YORAM SINGER

Yoram Singer was born in 1953 in Canada but spent most of his childhood in Switzerland. When Singer finished school he decided to travel to Israel to live and work. He started work in palliative care and felt that it was his calling to help the terminally ill. Singer believed in equality for all humans, no matter what their religion or ethnicity. His patience and compassion helped him grow in his role as a doctor.

Desert Angel

Singer was invited to run the palliative care unit at Ben-Gurion University's Faculty of Health Sciences. He accepted, knowing that he could do more for the ill there. He grew distressed by the lack of palliative care in the Negev desert so he decided to tend the terminally ill people there himself. He established the Bedouin Mobile Homecare Unit, which remains the only hospice care in the desert. More than 100,000 people live in the Negev desert and he realized that he needed additional help so he hired a translator to accompany him. Singer helped promote equality between the Bedouin and Jews as he felt that death is universal and people should not concentrate on differences and prejudices. He believed that all people have the right to dignity and grace at the end of their lives. Singer worked at his charity in his own time, and for no financial reward.

'The sadness of departing, the fear – not really of death, but of what's going to happen on the way and an urge to close circles, to say goodbye and to forgive. All these are quite universal. And if we could concentrate on our commonalities more than our differences, we would be much better off.'

Getting Creative

Singer was known to go out into appalling conditions to treat his patients, most of whom lived in tents and shacks in the Negev desert. His patients lived without electricity or running water. Health care was not accessible for these people as they had little transport or money. Singer made sure that no matter what the living conditions were that the care he provided would never suffer. He got creative with his medical methods and had been known to stand holding IV bags for patients. In places with no electricity, he would bring his own battery. Improvization was the key to Singer's work. He never became daunted by obstacles: he became even more determined.

Singer ignored religious differences and helped unite people with hope and optimism. He provided care for the dying every day. The care unit combined Western medicine with Bedouin culture and traditions. It was because of Singer's passion that the religious lines between Jewish and Bedouin patients were blurred and all patients, despite their religious beliefs could die with dignity. Singer remains active in care-giving and visits around 18,000 Bedouin patients a year, all of whom are poor and cannot afford medical care. He continues to find new, creative methods for his work too, always aware of the limited funds available. Singer lives his life out of the public eye but is truly committed to his patients. His patients regard him as an angel as he cares for the suffering and eases their transition into death.

Dr Yoram Singer.

ALBERTO CAIRO

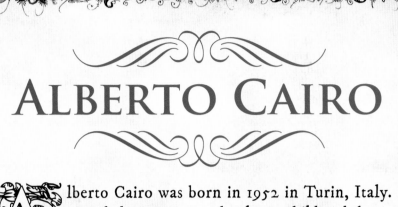

Alberto Cairo was born in 1952 in Turin, Italy. He attended a grammar school as a child and then went on to study law at Turin University. Cairo abandoned his career in law and retrained as a psychotherapist, a career in which he felt he could benefit others. Cairo worked at a hospital in Milan and then spent three years in Sudan. He later went on to Kabul, Afghanistan, to continue his charity work.

Charitable Work

Cairo arrived in Kabul in 1990 to run the orthopaedic rehabilitation programme there. The programme's main focus was to aid Afghans who were injured by over 30 years of warfare. It dealt mainly with amputees and equipped them with artificial limbs. Cairo was one of the first charity workers to arrive for the programme and was shocked by the vast amount of war casualties. He knew that it was his destiny to provide a better way of life for his patients. His charity did not end in just supplying artificial limbs for patients, he then went on to help them reintegrate into society. He frequently offered patients loans to start up businesses or gave them work in the rehabilitation centre. Cairo insisted on employing only people with disabilities to work for him. He believed that a centre for the disabled should be run by disabled people. He promoted positive discrimination and felt that his workers would act as positive role models for his patients.

'As a human being, I feel it is my duty to do something for other people in need. To believe or not to believe is something else, but I feel it is my duty to do something for people who are less fortunate, who are in bad situations.'

Angel of Kabul

Six centres were set up around Afghanistan for war casualties and by 1994, anyone with a motor disability was allowed to come in and be treated. Most of the patients were casualties of war, some victims of land mines and others were injured local civilians. Cairo headed the Kabul centre and felt it was his personal duty to see that as many patients as possible were treated. He saw over 300 patients daily and after their treatments, Cairo offered them counselling and training so they could progress in their lives. His dedication to his patients was awarded by the title 'Angel of Kabul'.

The orthopaedic rehabilitation programme is still active and since Cairo started working for the charity, over 50,000 people have received new limbs. Many of these patients return yearly for replacements or adjustments. Cairo has never believed in patient discrimination and has only ever asked for the name of his patients for records. Cairo aims to make people feel free to come to any of the centres for treatment, no matter what their political affiliation. He has treated wounded Taliban soldiers, police, children and war casualties. Cairo never discriminated as he saw all of his patients equally in need of his help. Every treatment offered in the centre was free, even lengthy treatments. Cairo was a candidate for the Nobel Peace Prize and wrote the bestselling book *Chroniques de Kaboul*. He has dedicated his life to giving back dignity and hope to the injured. He is a modern hero and is regarded as an earthy angel of Kabul.

'If you can improve the life of a person it gives you so much joy.'

Alberto Cairo speaks with a news correspondent on 15 November 2001 in Kabul, Afghanistan.

MOTHER TERESA

In 1910, Mother Teresa was born Agnes Gonxha Bojaxhiu in Skopje, Macedonia. She was the youngest of three children born to an Albanian builder. At 12 years old she was on a train journey when she felt a calling from God. The calling revealed that her duty and destiny was to spread the love of Christ. Throughout her childhood she immersed herself in prayers and the worship of God.

Charity Work

At 18 years old, Agnes left her home in Skopje to join the Sisters of Loreto in Ireland and become a Catholic nun. It was there that she decided to be known as Mother Teresa. After a little training, Mother Teresa was sent to India to do missionary work. She then began teaching at St Mary's High School for girls in Kolkata. However in 1948, she became increasingly disturbed by the suffering and poverty around her and was granted leave from the convent to work in the slums. The same year Mother Teresa left the convent she became an Indian citizen. She felt as though helping the poor and needy was answering her call from God, so she begun her work caring for the homeless, sick and dying. Mother Teresa had no income and had often to beg for food along with those she cared for. However, she was not tempted to go back to a comfortable life as she believed in her work. Even though she had no funds, Mother Teresa decided to open an open-air school for slum children and not long after, voluntary workers joined and funding support was offered. This was the beginning of what would turn into one of the greatest charity organizations ever.

On a Mission

In 1950, Mother Teresa gained permission to start her own order, The Missionaries of Charity. Their sole purpose was to look after the poorest and sickest people who were shunned by society and who others would not care for. Mother Teresa was concerned by the lack of health facilities such as hospitals and clinics for the poor so she quickly learnt medical techniques enabling her to treat those who could not afford medicine or doctors. This service inspired people to donate funds to her charity. The missionaries then went on to provide not only schools with health care but also shelters, orphanages and youth centres.

Mother Teresa then opened Kalighat Home for the Dying, an old Hindu temple converted into a free hospice for the poor to allow the dying to pass away with dignity and comfort. It did not discriminate and accepted people from all religions allowing them to spend their last days surrounded by love. Mother Teresa was a woman driven by a selfless need to help others. This was more evident than ever when she arranged a temporary ceasefire between the Palestinian guerrillas and the Israeli army so that she could rescue 37 children who were trapped in a front line hospital. She entered the war zone with great bravery to save the young and stranded which showed her boundless love for humanity. It was deeds like these that made this spiritual woman an international figure and world icon.

'Let us touch the dying, the poor, the lonely and the unwanted according to the graces we have received and let us not be ashamed or slow to do the humble work.'

Using the help from missionaries who had joined her, Mother Teresa expanded her centres for the poor and helpless all over the world. Her plans to create change were without limits and her desire to aid the needy grew. Mother Teresa's health centres then begun offering help for drug addicts, prostitutes and those suffering from incurable diseases. In 1985, her centre for those suffering with AIDS sheltered thousands of patients. In the 1990s, the charity had expanded to over 40 different countries and had over a million workers. Mother Teresa's divine efforts to promote peace, love and compassion all over the world was rewarded by her receiving many awards and distinctions, including the Padmashree Award from the President of India, the Order of Merit from Queen Elizabeth and the Pope John XXIII Peace Prize.

Final Years

Even in the last years of Mother Teresa's life, she served the poor and helped the sick and needy. She carried on despite her own ill heath and showed an unparalleled selflessness. By 1997, her charities had expanded to over 100 countries across the globe and she knew that her destiny had been fulfilled. She returned to Kolkata where she spent her last weeks instructing her successor and Sisters on how to proceed with the work she had started. She died in September 1997, a legend and leader for humanity. The Indian government granted her a state funeral to show gratitude towards her work for the poor and sick who she cared for no matter their background.

Divine Capabilities

Mother Teresa was not just a devoted woman of God and mother to the needy but she was also thought of as an angel. Monica Bestra, a sick woman suffering from a tumour in her abdomen, claimed that a beam of light that emanated from a picture of Mother Teresa in her locket had cured her cancerous tumour, a claim which portrayed Mother Teresa as a saint with divine capabilities. This miracle was documented as a step towards possible canonisation. In 2003, Pope John Paul II beatified Mother Teresa in Rome, which marked the first step of her sainthood.

Mother Teresa was not just a dedicated humanitarian; she was also an ambassador for change. She taught the way of God and the importance of helping others. She was not just a mother to the poor but also a mother to all humans, teaching them the significance of love and compassion for all people, no matter what their social position, religion or health. She marked a new age in charity and her legacy will undoubtedly live on forever along with her advice:

'Never travel faster than your guardian angel can fly.'

Mother Teresa cradling an infant in Kolkata, India.

ELIZABETH FRY

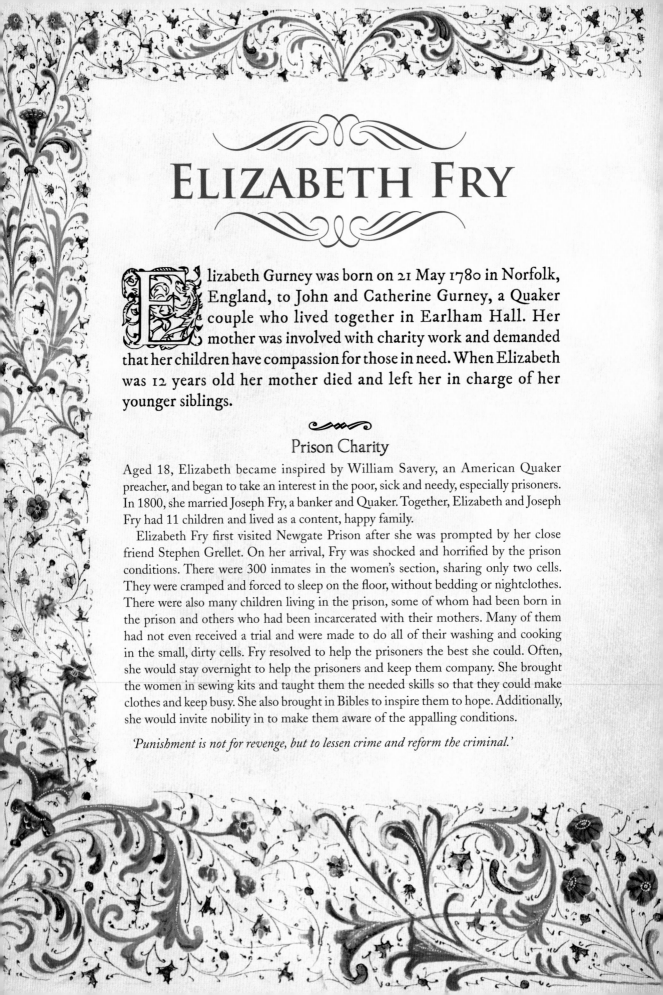

Elizabeth Gurney was born on 21 May 1780 in Norfolk, England, to John and Catherine Gurney, a Quaker couple who lived together in Earlham Hall. Her mother was involved with charity work and demanded that her children have compassion for those in need. When Elizabeth was 12 years old her mother died and left her in charge of her younger siblings.

Prison Charity

Aged 18, Elizabeth became inspired by William Savery, an American Quaker preacher, and began to take an interest in the poor, sick and needy, especially prisoners. In 1800, she married Joseph Fry, a banker and Quaker. Together, Elizabeth and Joseph Fry had 11 children and lived as a content, happy family.

Elizabeth Fry first visited Newgate Prison after she was prompted by her close friend Stephen Grellet. On her arrival, Fry was shocked and horrified by the prison conditions. There were 300 inmates in the women's section, sharing only two cells. They were cramped and forced to sleep on the floor, without bedding or nightclothes. There were also many children living in the prison, some of whom had been born in the prison and others who had been incarcerated with their mothers. Many of them had not even received a trial and were made to do all of their washing and cooking in the small, dirty cells. Fry resolved to help the prisoners the best she could. Often, she would stay overnight to help the prisoners and keep them company. She brought the women in sewing kits and taught them the needed skills so that they could make clothes and keep busy. She also brought in Bibles to inspire them to hope. Additionally, she would invite nobility in to make them aware of the appalling conditions.

'Punishment is not for revenge, but to lessen crime and reform the criminal.'

Fry began to have financial and personal difficulties at home. Elizabeth and Joseph Fry's daughter Betsy died at five years old, leaving the family distraught. The Fry bank was also suffering, leaving the family with financial worries. In 1816, after some time out to tend to her family, Fry went back to Newgate prison to start a prison school for the children there. She then went on to establish the first nationwide women's organization, the British Ladies' Society for Promoting the Reformation of Female Prisoners. This was not the only organization she formed; she was also active in forming the Association for the Reformation of the Female Prisoners in Newgate. Fry was determined in her struggle to help improve the lives of prisoners and seemed to be their only hope. People were amazed by Fry's heart and devotion. They believed her to be miraculous, a gift sent from the heavens.

'I have seen Elizabeth Fry in Newgate and I have witnessed there miraculous effects of true Christianity upon the most depraved of human beings.'

Flying in the Face of Criticism

However, Fry's work did not go without criticism. She was often accused of being a bad mother and wife because she dedicated her life to humanitarian charity. People could not understand her selflessness but Fry was willing to self-sacrifice to help the countless needy. Lord Sidmouth, an MP, was unsympathetic towards Fry's cause as he felt that if the prison conditions improved, crime would increase as people would not fear incarceration. His views were naïve to the fact that many people who were incarcerated had not been given a trial and therefore had not been proven guilty. A high number of prisoners were held for petty crimes or accused of crimes that they had not committed. Fry ignored Sidmouth's ignorance as she knew the truth behind her cause. She was determined and all criticism made her strive harder for results.

An Inspired Humanitarian

Fry had compassion for all needy people, not just prisoners. In addition to her charity at the prison, she also ran a night shelter for the homeless. This idea was prompted after she saw the lifeless body of a young boy on the street. She could not fathom how people could be so indifferent and cold-hearted. In 1824, during a holiday to Brighton, East Sussex, Fry founded the Brighton District Visiting Society. This organization employed volunteers to aid the poor in their homes and tend to the needy. This organization did not end in Brighton; it spread throughout other districts and was a huge success.

Fry also started a training school for nurses at Guy's Hospital in London as she felt that the nurses were not trained properly. The Fry nurses had their own uniform and not only tended to patients' physical needs but also their spiritual needs. This was what later influenced Florence Nightingale to help nurses train. Nightingale wrote expressing her admiration for Fry's work in the hospital. Later, Nightingale took Fry nurses with her when she went to the Crimean War. Again, Fry proved what an inspiration she was as her work influenced other people who went on to become influential humanitarians.

As years went on, Fry got a reputation for her kindness. Men sought her for professional advice which was extremely uncommon at the time. Queen Victoria was an admirer and donated funds to her cause. In 1828, Joseph Fry's business deteriorated further and he was declared bankrupt. It was Elizabeth Fry's brother-in-law Thomas Fowell Buxton who came to her aid. Buxton could not stand letting all her hard work and charity fail so became her business manager and benefactor. With his help and financial input, Fry's charity expanded. Buxton was elected to parliament, providing Fry with a platform to promote her charity. His fellow MPs assisted Buxton and Fry, supporting their cause. Fry gave evidence to the House of Commons committee regarding the appalling prison conditions. She became the first woman to give evidence in parliament, a huge step for female equality.

Remembering an Angel

Fry died in 1845 from a stroke. She was buried in the Friends' burial ground at Barking, with over a thousand attendees gathered in silence. As a mark of respect for Fry, the Seamen of the Ramsgate Coast Guard flew their flag at half mast. Until then, this had only been done for dead members of the ruling monarchy. The Lord Mayor of London held a meeting in regards to creating a refuge home for the needy in memory of Fry. Four years later, the first Elizabeth Fry refuge opened its doors. Fry was widely recognized for her achievements and will always be remembered for being a devoted humanitarian and an earthly angel.

Elizabeth Fry visiting inmates in Newgate Prison, London.

SUSAN ALDOUS

Susan Aldous was born in 1961 in Australia and was raised by foster parents in Melbourne. She was an unruly child with a wild spirit. As a teenager in the 1970s, she dropped out of school and involved herself with bikers, getting tattoos and living life in the fast lane. She became pre-occupied with drugs and rebelled against authority. Despite her choice of lifestyle, she was always compassionate towards others.

Susan soon realized that she needed to change her lifestyle. During a walk around the red light district in Melbourne, she had an epiphany. She encountered members of Christian groups who were helping the needy. They explained to her the importance of life and she realized that she was meant for something extraordinary. After this, she noted that her new 'drug of choice' was compassion.

> 'When I was five my grandmother told me about the courageous Joan of Arc responding to the angel's voice, so I knew that women were every bit as brave as men. I believed that one day I would be called by the angels to undertake a special and difficult mission.'

Angel of Bang Kwang

Aldous spent nine days in Thailand during her volunteering project in Southeast Asian slums and prisons. Once she saw the abandonment and poor living conditions of Thai prisoners she decided to stay. Chavoret Jaruboon, a close friend of Aldous worked as a senior guard at Bang Kwang prison. They were unlikely allies as Jaruboon's job was to execute condemned prisoners with a submachine gun. Despite his career choice, he was instrumental in helping Susan change the living conditions of the inmates. The

prisoners named the duo the 'angel and the devil'. However, Jaruboon displayed kindness towards inmates which went unrecognized. When Aldous initially decided to help improve the lives of inmates, it was Jaruboon who voiced the idea of eyeglasses for poor, elderly prisoners. Susan acted on her friend's advice and provided glasses for more than 150 elderly prisoners. Aldous's charity expanded throughout the prison and Jaruboon continued to help her on her quest for change. Aldous stated that it was never her intention to rid the prisoners of their sentences as many were dangerous criminals who were convicted of murderous acts, she simply felt it was not humane for the prisoners to be completely abandoned in the system. She remained the prisoners' only source of empathy and understanding, and to the many who were facing death, their only hope lay in the angelic Susan Aldous.

Charity

Over the years, Aldous dedicated her life to helping others. She not only helped those in confinement, she also helped prostitutes, the terminally ill, refugees, drug addicts and disabled children. Aldous wanted her life to have meaning after spending her teenage years alone; she found this in helping others, the only thing that brought her true happiness. Susan wrote the acclaimed novel *The Angel of Bang Kwang Prison*. Here she recounted her transformative journey helping those in Thai prisons. Through her novel, she gave voice to those who were left to rot with no dignity and who were robbed of basic human rights and compassion. Aldous proved that she was not just another idealist; she was determined to bring about real change. She has never claimed to be a saint, but her charity and compassion made her deserving of the title 'Angel of Bang Kwang'.

Susan Aldous with two inmates of Bang Kwang Prison.

OSKAR SCHINDLER

Oskar Schindler was born on 28 April 1908 in Zwittau, Moravia. At the time, Moravia was a German province of the Austro-Hungarian Empire, now part of the Czech Republic. Oskar's father Hans Schindler was a factory owner and his mother Louisa Schindler, a housewife. Oskar Schindler had a privileged childhood and was brought up as a German catholic.

Oskar was a popular child and befriended two boys who were sons of a local rabbi. In the 1920s, he went to work for his father and in 1928, married Emilie Pelzl. His marriage caused a rift with his father so he left his employment and travelled to Poland. In the 1930s, as a result of the economic depression, the Schindler business became bankrupt.

In 1933, Adolf Hitler assumed the post of chancellor in Germany. Schindler, along with other Sudeten Germans, joined the pro-Nazi Sudeten German Party. Schindler did not join out of agreement with the Nazis, but as a means to develop himself as a businessman. Under Hitler's rule, Germany annexed Sudetenland and in 1939, invaded Poland, prompting World War II.

Wartime Black Market Business

During Germany's invasion of Poland, Schindler moved to Krakow. He created friendships with key officers in the German army and the Nazi SS. He used these friendships to create a black market business which sold illegal goods such as cigars and alcohol. In 1940, Schindler brought a kitchen factory which he later named Emalia. He then hired Itzhak Stern, a clever Jewish accountant to work for him. It was through Stern that he reached out to the Jewish community for workers. At the

time, Jewish people in Krakow were poor and victimized, mostly living in ghettos reserved for Jews. With Stern's help, Schindler employed 250 Poles and seven Jews. Over the next two years the number grew significantly to 370 Jews and 430 Poles. The German army believed that Schindler was employing so many Jews for cheap labour. However, his motives were very different, as is evident in the following quote:

'I was now resolved to do everything in my power to defeat the system.'

Schindler's financial success earned him respect among the SS parties and his relationships with high ranking officers improved. However, he had a low opinion of the Nazis and was disgusted by their brutal treatment of the Jews. He used his relationships with officers to cover his true intent. Schindler decided that he wanted to help his Jewish workers to be free from brutality. When the Germans sent out for his employees to be deported, Schindler raced down to the train station to claim exemptions for them. He not only employed healthy men to work but also women, children and handicapped people. He claimed that they were all important workers in his factory and name-dropped some of his high ranking Nazi friends to strengthen his claim. These claims were what saved the workers from being sent to concentration camps where they would be murdered. Schindler rescued his workers and brought them back to the factory where they were safe.

The Rescue

In 1943, the SS arranged for the final liquidation of the Krakow ghetto, and the remaining Jews were categorized into groups. Those who were strong and healthy enough to work were sent to the Plaszow forced labour camp. All other Jews were either executed on the spot or sent to death camps. This sickened Schindler so he bribed Amon Goeth, the SS officer in charge of the operation, to allow him to establish a labour mini-camp within his factory where he

Oskar Schindler visiting Israel in 1962.

would carry on employing Jewish workers. He employed another 1,000 Jewish workers and let 450 local Jews who were working at nearby labour camps sleep overnight in his factory. The workers wages were ordered to be sent to the SS, leaving the workers poor. Schindler could not leave his workers helpless and provided them all with food and shelter. News of Schindler's kindness towards the Jews echoed throughout the cities which led to him getting arrested three times and being accused of aiding Jews without authorization. He was also accused of corrupting Jewish employees but the SS and police were unable to charge him. Schindler carried on despite the accusations and personal risk.

A year later, the Plaszow labour camp was turned into another concentration camp. All of the prisoners kept there were sent to be executed. Schindler's full factory was then told that they would have to close and that all the workers must go to the death camps. Schindler fought against this and bribed Goeth again to let him move his factory to Brunnlitz, Moravia. He told officials that he could not close the factory as it supplied vital war supplies to Hitler's army. This excuse sufficed but Schindler was told he had to draw up a list of the names of the people who he would take with him. This task pained him as he had spent years rescuing Jews and now had to choose who was to live or die. The final list contained 1,100 names, some being employees and others friends. The list of these names came to be known as 'Schindler's list'. Late in 1944, Schindler made the final necessary bribes to move his factory and 800 of his workers were shipped out to Brunnlitz. The remaining 300 women and children who were supposed to join them were mistakenly sent to Auschwitz death camp. Schindler was horrified and set out to rescue them. He was successful with the rescue and the remaining Jews were sent to Brunnlitz to join the others.

'Now you are finally with me, you are safe now. Don't be afraid of anything. You don't have to worry anymore.'

The Final Save

At the end of the war, a train containing 120 evacuated people from Goleszow camp was left stranded in Svitavy. They were all near death after being in the train for a week without food or water. Schindler contacted the SS and told them that he needed these people to work in his factory. His request was granted but 13 of the rescued people were already dead by the time he reached them. The others were safely sent to the factory. The 13 dead were not cremated but buried because Schindler wanted to respect their Jewish tradition. Schindler presented bogus figures to officials so that they would believe his factory to be active. He only actually produced one wagon full of ammunition in nearly a year. The business was a failure but the true charity behind the illusion was a success and over 1,000 Jews were saved.

Post War Legacy

After the war ended, Schindler and his wife emigrated to South America. Schindler returned to Germany alone in 1957, having separated from his wife. He was awarded the title Righteous among the Nations as recognition of his efforts to save Jews during the Holocaust. Schindler was bankrupt as he had spent every penny paying bribes and funding factories in order to save lives. He died in 1974, and his body was transferred to Israel for burial. In 1993, Emilie Schindler accepted the Medal of Remembrance on Schindler's behalf. This rare medal noted Schindler's heroic achievements during the Holocaust. Schindler spent many years buying the lives of Jews and never faltered in his mission. Because of his purity and compassion, Schindler will always be remembered as an earthly angel to the Jews and protector of humanity.

ANGELS OF BATAAN

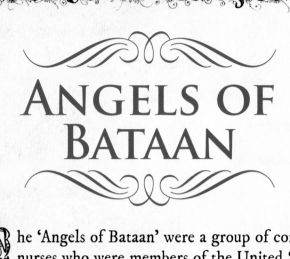

The 'Angels of Bataan' were a group of compassionate nurses who were members of the United States Army Nurse Corps and the United States Navy Nurse Corps. During World War II, they were sent to Manila in the Philippines and put to work in Sternberg General Hospital. The wards were infested with malaria and constantly under fire.

During the Battle of the Philippines in 1941, the conditions within the hospital deteriorated and the nurses' workload increased dramatically. The Japanese invasion of Manila sent many casualties flooding into Sternberg hospital but there were so few beds that many had to be treated on the floor. Off-duty nurses and civilians were also brought in to assist. After the US surrendered to the Japanese, 66 US army nurses were forced by the army to flee to Bataan and the Malinta tunnel on the island of Corregidor. The navy nurses stayed behind in Manila to support the patients through the initial invasions. These nurses were led by Laura M Cobb who was determined to fight for her patients. During the invasion, 11 of the navy nurses were captured and taken to Santo Tomas internment camp by the Japanese. However, one navy nurse named Ann A Bernatitus escaped to Bataan. Bernatitus joined with the army nurses who were under the command of Captain Maude Davison. Together, the escapees were evacuated on a submarine. They served in the Battle of Bataan and the Battle of Corregidor. During these battles, other nurses including Captain Maude Davison were captured and imprisoned by the Japanese.

Angel of Mercy

Ann A Bernatitus was 29 years old when she fled from Manila. She was a nurse who had joined the navy to improve her life and gain status. At the time, women were not treated as equals with men. Bernatitus enjoyed being addressed as 'miss' and felt as though she was doing something constructive with her life. In 1941, Bernatitus and the other nurses were made aware of the attack on Pearl Harbor and knew that the Philippines would be next. Despite the threat, the nurses went back to their duties and carried on aiding the needy. After the initial attack, Bernatitus and the army nurses travelled to the Bataan Peninsula to safety. Bernatitus, alongside other nurses, worked hard on the front line, giving aid to troops. Initially Bernatitus was stationed at hospital one in camp Limay. The hospital then moved further down the peninsula and the Japanese bombed it, killing many already injured soldiers. Bataan soon fell to the Japanese and the remaining 79,000 soldiers were sent to do the infamous death march. Bernatitus, along with some other nurses, managed to escape to Corregidor. With Bataan and Manila taken over, the Japanese set their full force on the small island of Corregidor. Bernatitus was the only navy nurse to escape Corregidor and was later named the 'angel of mercy'.

'In those days we were neither fish nor fowl. We were not officers and we were not enlisted. We were in between. We did not get the pay of an officer but we got more than the enlisted.'

Santo Tomas Internment

When the Japanese invaded Manila, Bataan and Corregidor, the captured nurses were sent to Santo Tomas internment camp. They were led by Captain Maude Davison who commanded them to wear their Red Cross bands so the prisoners would know that they would aid and assist. They were offered hot drinks but refused out of fear of being poisoned. The nurses were not defeated though and began to treat wounded soldiers within the camp. Over the three years of internment, the nurses lost weight and suffered malnutrition. The food sources were scarce and all prisoners were rationed less than half of the food they needed to be healthy. They feared that they would never get out alive but back in the US the news of these remarkable women travelled. American Major General Vernon Mudge led an aggressive raid on the camp and on 3 February 1945, the nurses and other internees were liberated by US forces.

CAPTAIN MAUDE DAVISON

Captain Maude Davison was an army nurse commander who led the nurses at Bataan and Corregidor. Her leadership and tenderness continued even when she was incarcerated at Santo Tomas. Davison was 58 years old when she was taken as a prisoner of war. During her time in Santo Tomas camp, Davison carried on with duties as chief nurse and offered support and kindness to her fellow nurses and prisoners. Her health deteriorated dramatically while she was imprisoned, causing her body weight to drop by half. Once liberated, Davison had to be hospitalized immediately. It touched many that Davison, even in ill health, remained selfless and righteous. She never complained, she just got on with her work and set aside her own personal fears, displaying the image of a calm, composed woman. Even in the bleakest, most hopeless moments she inspired the other nurses. After liberation in 1947, Davison married Dr Charles Jackson. She died in 1956, at age 71. In recognition of her work she was awarded the Distinguished Service Medal by the President of the USA. Memorials were held in her name, recognizing Davison as the leader of the Angels of Bataan.

Recognition

The nurses who survived the dreadful years of incarceration stuck together and showed strength and unity. It was because of this that they managed to survive the horrendous camp. In 1980, a plaque was hung at the Mount Samat shrine. It was in remembrance of the brave angels who endured the bombings and starvation and still returned to their duties. Not only are they American heroes, they are also angels, a title which was well earned.

'Their hearts were the same hearts as those of the women of early America. Their names must always be hallowed when we speak of American heroes. The memory of their coming ashore on Corregidor that early morning of April 9, 1942 dirty, dishevelled, some of them wounded from the hospital bombings – and every last one of them with her chin up in the air.'

The Angels of Bataan leaving Santo Tomas.

HISTORICAL ANGELS

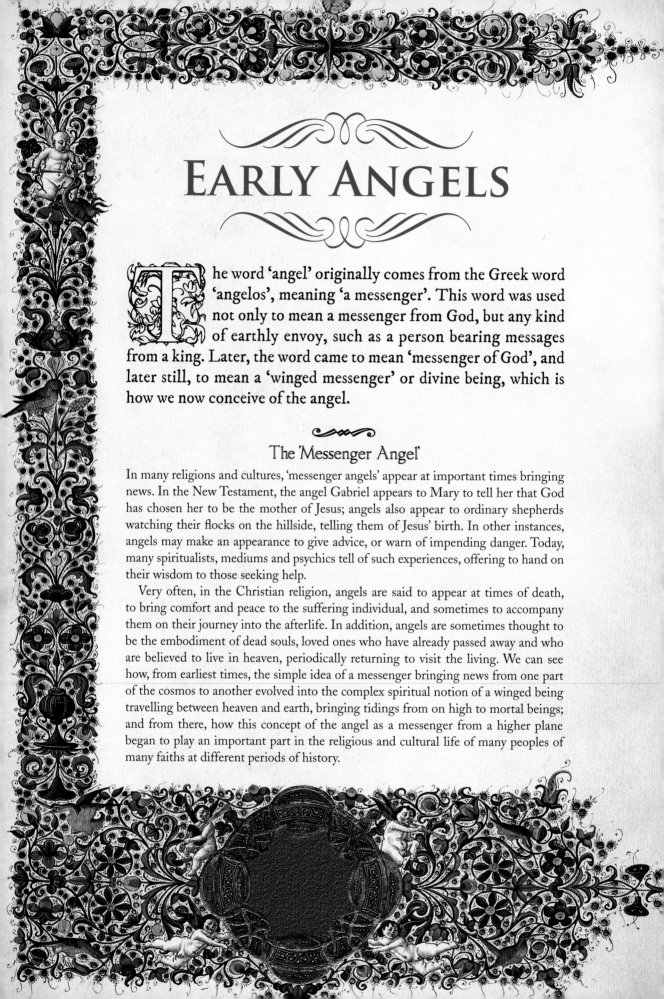

EARLY ANGELS

The word 'angel' originally comes from the Greek word 'angelos', meaning 'a messenger'. This word was used not only to mean a messenger from God, but any kind of earthly envoy, such as a person bearing messages from a king. Later, the word came to mean 'messenger of God', and later still, to mean a 'winged messenger' or divine being, which is how we now conceive of the angel.

The 'Messenger Angel'

In many religions and cultures, 'messenger angels' appear at important times bringing news. In the New Testament, the angel Gabriel appears to Mary to tell her that God has chosen her to be the mother of Jesus; angels also appear to ordinary shepherds watching their flocks on the hillside, telling them of Jesus' birth. In other instances, angels may make an appearance to give advice, or warn of impending danger. Today, many spiritualists, mediums and psychics tell of such experiences, offering to hand on their wisdom to those seeking help.

Very often, in the Christian religion, angels are said to appear at times of death, to bring comfort and peace to the suffering individual, and sometimes to accompany them on their journey into the afterlife. In addition, angels are sometimes thought to be the embodiment of dead souls, loved ones who have already passed away and who are believed to live in heaven, periodically returning to visit the living. We can see how, from earliest times, the simple idea of a messenger bringing news from one part of the cosmos to another evolved into the complex spiritual notion of a winged being travelling between heaven and earth, bringing tidings from on high to mortal beings; and from there, how this concept of the angel as a messenger from a higher plane began to play an important part in the religious and cultural life of many peoples of many faiths at different periods of history.

The Annunciation, School of Jean Fouquet, c.1465.

Angelology — the Study of Angels

The study of angels is known as 'angelology'. Today, angelologists are scholars of theology, who study the Bible, in particular the descriptions of angels given in *Ezekiel*, *Revelation*, and ancient texts such as the *Book of Enoch*. Angelologists also include contemporary mystics and spiritualists who base their knowledge and practice on a number of other sources, whether their own visions, biblical texts, ancient pagan cults, or other religions such as Buddhism.

Our modern idea of the angel, as we shall see, is rooted in many cultures across the world, both past and present. The image of a beautiful, human-like being with wings — part human, and part divine — is largely derived from Judaism, but it also goes back many years before that, to Neolithic times. Winged angels were also depicted in early civilizations such as Sumeria, Ancient Egypt, and Persia.

The Guardian Angel

In Western culture today, angels are usually seen as good and kind, as benefactors to humanity. They are conceived of as superhuman beings with special powers that they use to protect us, fighting against demons and other evil spirits. This idea comes from antiquity, where we find many stories of guardian angels assigned by God or other deities to guard and teach a particular individual on earth.

The guardian angel of these early myths and stories would, characteristically, also pray to God to help the individual, pleading his or her case in times of trouble or wrongdoing. Over the centuries, the concept of the guardian angel, with special responsibility for a person under their care, became especially strong in the Catholic religion. However, variants of it can be found in many other mythologies, including pagan and new-age belief systems.

Lucifer, the 'Fallen Angel'

Not all angels are good and kind, however. An important section of Christian theology is devoted to stories of 'fallen angels' — angels who have been banished from heaven for wrongdoing. The most famous of these is Lucifer, whose name means 'light bearer' in Latin, and originally signified the appearance of the morning star, the first star to come out in the sky at dawn.

In some versions of the story, Lucifer remains a positive force, simply as 'the light bearer' angel. However, in the Christian religion, following a passage in the *Book of Isaiah*, Lucifer becomes synonymous with the Devil. Continuing this line of interpretation, Milton's epic 17th-century poem *Paradise Lost* tells the story of the War in Heaven (first described in the Bible, in the *Book of Revelation*). According to this account, the leader of the rebel angels, Lucifer, loses the war, and is consequently cast out of heaven into hell, becoming the ruler of the underworld. As Satan or the devil, he is in command of all manner of evil demons and spirits, and continues his battle against God and the forces of good in the world.

Today, there is some dispute in theological circles as to whether Satan and Lucifer are, in Christian terms, one and the same. It has been pointed out that there is no reference to Satan as Lucifer in the New Testament, and some leading scholars argue that the two are quite separate beings. However, the story of Lucifer, the fallen angel, being expelled from heaven and taking his revenge as Satan, lord of the underworld, has had a powerful grip on the Western imagination since Milton's retelling of the story in his masterwork, *Paradise Lost*.

Shaman Culture

The idea of a human-like being with wings, able to fly between the earthly and spiritual realms, has been traced way back in time to the Shamanic beliefs of Central Asia in the Neolithic period. Shamanism is a primitive belief system that occurs in many cultures, and is essentially the idea that a specially gifted human individual, known as a 'Shaman', can communicate with the spirit world, bringing back messages for the community, usually for their benefit. The Shaman's function is often to solve difficult problems, such as disputes over territory, and to alleviate pain or sickness, whether of the soul or the body. Shamanism is found all over the world, at all periods in history, and still continues to be practised in many countries today. Significantly, Shamans in all these cultures are said to have a special, superhuman power – the ability, like angels, to fly.

THE NEOLITHIC PERIOD

In Anatolia, Turkey, a village called Catal Huyuk has, since the 1960s, been in the process of excavation, and has yielded very exciting archeological finds from the period dating 6,500 BC. Mud huts have been discovered, with hatches in the roofs, through which the villagers are thought to have entered. Bones of the dead have been found under platforms inside the houses, suggesting that these people left the corpses of relatives outside to be eaten by vultures.

There is no exact record of the beliefs of the people of Catal Huyuk, but religious ceremonies obviously played a central part in the villagers' lives. Among the artefacts found at the site were figurines made of clay and stone, showing worship of the prehistoric mother goddess, and of the veneration of the bull. These cults are found in other early civilizations as well. Most importantly, for our story of the angel, was evidence of an extraordinary, somewhat sinister 'vulture cult'. Vulture skulls were found on the walls of the houses, covered in plaster in the shape of human breasts, the beak of the vulture forming the nipple. In one room, which became known as the 'vulture shrine', a figure of a human being in a vulture skin, with vulture wings, was drawn on the wall; it was biting the head off a human body.

The Vulture Cult

Next, archeologists discovered the skulls of large predatory birds, including eagles and vultures – the bearded vulture and the griffon vulture – laid out in what appeared to be a pattern. The wing bones were not present, suggesting that the wings may have been taken off and used as costumes in some kind of religious ritual or ceremony.

Of course, the meaning of these finds remains shrouded in mystery. It seems likely that these early people believed that donning the vulture wings would give them special powers – perhaps the ability to fly, but also to mediate between the earthly and spiritual realm. The biting off of the human head by the winged half-bird, half-human creature might also signify the Shaman's ability to send the deceased soul on its way into the afterlife. In this sense, the magical human/vulture hybrid may have been the first image of the angel in human civilization.

Vulture Worship

Whatever the exact meaning of the mystery, it seems that the vulture cult was an early representation of the idea that a winged messenger could travel between the human and spirit world – especially when we find that vultures, in many civilizations have been venerated (as well as feared) as 'purifiers': birds who clean up the landscape, making it fit for human habitation. In many parts of the world, the vulture was also respected because it refrained from killing any other living creature, waiting until it was dead before eating it. It was also praised for living peacefully in large communal flocks, sharing its meals with others.

Thus, the largely negative image of the vulture in modern Western culture as a sinister scavenger is at odds with that of many early peoples in hot climates, who were grateful to the bird for getting rid of diseased corpses, whether human or animal, left to rot in the sun. It is a fact that even dead animals infected with botulism and anthrax

Christ Surrounded by Two Angels, St. Vitalis and Bishop Ecclesius, Byzantine School, *c.*6th century.

can be safely consumed by the vulture, owing to the bird's corrosive stomach acids. This meant that human communities living with vultures in the area would be protected from serious infectious diseases, which is perhaps part of the reason that the birds were welcomed and worshipped, at that time, as spirit beings – even, possibly angels – albeit of a rather unusual kind.

The Peacock Angel

Today, a group of people known as the Yazidi, today living in reduced numbers mostly in Iraq, but formerly in large communities in Turkey, Armenia and Syria, continue the tradition of worshipping a bird as an angel. The Yazidi believe that God created the world and placed it under the care of seven angels. The most important of these angels is Melek Taus, who takes the form of a peacock.

Melek Taus is known by another name, Shaytan, in the Qur'an, which is also the Muslim word for Satan, or the Devil. For this reason, Muslims and Christians have often mistakenly believed that the Yazidi are devil worshippers, though this is not the case. In the Yazidi creation myth, God created Melek Taus from his own image, and went on to create the other six archangels. The archangels were sent to earth to collect dust, from which God built the body of Adam and gave it life by breathing into it. God ordered all the archangels to bow to Adam and obey him, which they did, except Melek Taus, who argued that as he was created in God's own image, he should not bow to anyone. God agreed with him, and made him chief of the angels, and his representative on earth.

The Angakkuq

In northern Asia, particularly Siberia, Shamanism continues to this day. Central to many Shaman rituals is the donning of costumes representing birds – birds being the main spirit protectors of the Shaman.

In the Inuit tribe, the Shaman often wore a coat with long fringes along the lower edge of the sleeves and along the bottom, symbolizing bird feathers. On the back of the coat might be a bird, such as a grouse, the vital force of the Shaman, and a bear, said to be the Shaman's assistant. Other features of the coat would include tubular metal pendants, indicating the 'voices' of the spirits, round pendants on the shoulders, which were solar signs, and square ones, symbolizing passage to the lower world. Twisted strands of reindeer hair on the side of the coat indicated the Shaman's special routes into the spiritual world.

The Shaman, known as the angakkuq, was a very important person in the Inuit community. He or she would be relied on to interpret the world of spirits for the benefit of the community. The Shaman was not trained, but rather chosen for his or her natural abilities, which would be recognized in the child as it grew up. The Shaman acted as a medical doctor, tending wounds, and as a psychic healer, offering advice and invoking the spirits to help individuals in their lives. The Inuit believe that all creatures, including animals, have souls, and that even when hunting animals, respect must be paid to them and the proper rituals observed. If this was not done, the spirit of the animal or bird, once liberated through death, would take revenge on the huntsmen. This is why animals, and in particular, birds, were treated by the Inuit as spiritual beings on a par with humans.

SUMERIAN ANGELS

While evidence of winged human figures can be found in Neolithic culture and in ancient Shamanic belief systems, our first really clear picture of the angel comes in a series of Sumerian stone relief carvings dating from around 3,000 BC. Sumerian civilization existed in present-day Iraq, in the area between the Tigris and Euphrates rivers.

The Sumerians worshipped a number of gods and spirits, including Anu, the sky god, Ki, the earth god, Utu, the sun god, and Nanna, the moon god. Other deities, such as the morning star Innana, Enki the god of plenty, and Enlil, lord of the ghost land, were also part of the Sumerian cosmogony. In addition, the Sumerians believed in a group of winged messengers, who were able to fly very fast, and who ran errands between the deities and the humans.

Each of the Sumerian deities was worshipped in a different city across a large empire, and their powers were thought to wax and wane according to the fortunes of the cities they belonged to. Therefore, the messenger angels became very important in communicating between the various gods and cities. The Sumerians believed that each individual person had a 'ghost' attached to them – an entity that became a companion to them throughout life, often helping them when they ran into difficulties. Nowadays, we might express this role as a 'guardian angel'. Archeologists have found altars erected to these guardian angels in ancient Sumerian buildings, some of them with wall paintings and engravings of winged human figures.

It is possible that the Sumerians might have derived their belief in the 'messenger' and 'guardian' angels from ancient Shamanistic belief systems. It is also likely that when the Sumerian civilization was conquered by Semitic tribes, in around 1,900 BC, the victors borrowed the idea of winged messenger and guardian spirits – angels – from the Sumerians, and began to use it in a new way. These Semitic tribes had many gods, and accordingly, developed the idea of a whole corpus of angels, divided into ranks, serving different gods. This came to be a cornerstone of later religious systems, such as Zoroastrianism (see pages 79-80) and Judaism, where only one god was worshipped.

ANCIENT EGYPT

The civilization of Ancient Egypt lasted over three millennia, starting in 3,150 BC and ending in 31 BC when it fell to the Roman empire. It was a highly sophisticated culture, making huge advances in agriculture, technology, and the arts. The pharaoh, or king, was believed to rule by divine right, and could call on a host of gods and goddesses with supernatural powers to help him. The gods also ruled the daily life of ordinary people, and had to be appeased with offerings and prayers.

As in Shamanic belief systems, the Ancient Egyptians considered the phenomena of nature, whether the elements or the animal kingdom, to be divine forces. They accorded each of these a god or goddess, in a very complex system which was constantly altered and added to. Thus, there might be several kinds of contradictory mythologies that were all held to be true at once. The Egyptians saw this as reflecting the variety of human experience, rather than as problematic. In addition, they tended to depict the gods and goddesses in various forms, believing that the true nature of the deities was deeply mysterious. For this reason, the same god or goddess might be characterized in many different ways.

Isis, the Winged Goddess

One such deity was Isis, the great mother goddess, who had magical powers but was also good and warm-hearted. She was worshipped as the goddess of simplicity. Isis was the daughter of Geb, the god of the earth, and Nut, the goddess of the sky. In some myths, she conceived a child, Horus, with her brother, Osiris, whom she later saved from death with her magic powers.

Early pictures of Isis show her as wearing a long, sheath dress and holding a lotus. In later versions, she assumes some of the roles of Hathor,

Ancient Egyptian depiction of the Goddess Isis.

another fertility goddess, who traditionally wears the horns of a cow on her head. Other images show her holding her son, Horus, with a crown, a vulture, an owl, and other birds. She sometimes has a large set of wings attached to her lower arms, giving her the appearance of an angel, and in some instances, is represented as a kite flying above the body of Osiris, her dead husband.

Isis has many different roles in Ancient Egyptian religion; she uses her magical powers to heal, and her wings to enfold her subjects in sleep. She may also appear as an angel to those who are coming to the end of their lives. She was such a powerful goddess in this far-reaching civilization that she went on to be worshipped, in many different forms, throughout the Graeco-Roman world for many years, until the suppression of paganism by Christianity. In some traditions, she became incorporated into Judaism, and – taking up her history as a winged goddess of heaven – was worshipped as a Seraph (see page 84).

The Hunmanit

The Hunmanit, in Ancient Egyptian religion, were a group of beings connected with the sun. They were imagined as rays of the sun, similar to the Christian image of the angel choir. The Hunmanit were servants to the gods, with a responsibility to look after the sun. For this reason, they were important also to human beings, who depended on the sun for growing crops. In their role as winged beings, and as guardians, they were the forerunners to the Christian concepts of the heavenly choir of angels, and the guardian angel, that we know today.

The Mithraic Mysteries

This mystery cult, which is thought to have flourished from around 1,500 BC and later became popular among the Persians and Romans, centred around the god Mithras, the light bringer. Believed to have been born from a rock,

Mithras was often depicted sacrificing a bull. In these images, his cloak billows out behind him, suggesting wings. The disciples of Mithras met in underground temples, many of which still survive, and are believed to have undergone complex initiation rites. Other than that, little is known about the cult.

In many instances, throughout antiquity, Mithras is called the sun god. He is typically seen as embodying love, friendship, kindness, and mercy. The idea of him being a messenger, or an angel, mediating between heaven and earth, also crops up in several religions, including Zoroastrianism. Mithras also appears in sacred Hindu texts as Mitra, where he is mentioned many times (for example in the Sanskrit *Rigveda*), and, in his Persian form, is known as 'Mihr' or 'Mehr'.

THE PROPHET ZOROASTER

The ancient Iranian prophet Zoroaster (also known as Zarathustra), is thought to have lived around the time of the 10th century BC. Zoroaster was a member of a migrant Indo-European community living in present day Iran. He founded the Zoroastrian religion, which – in a very modern way – focuses not just on worship of a deity, but on the human condition and our constant struggle to live according to 'asa' (the truth) rather than 'druj' (the lie).

Zoroaster's teachings were eventually adopted as the religion of the Persian empire, and later influenced philosophical and religious thought in many cultures, including Greek, Roman, Jewish, Islamic, and Christian. Many different, and often contradictory, qualities came to be attributed to Zoroaster. The ancient Greeks held him to be the inventor of sorcery and magic; however, in the post-classical era he was seen by such philosophers as Voltaire and Nietzsche as promoting a more rational, enlightened form of belief in God.

Zoroaster's Visions

Zoroaster proclaimed that God, whom he saw as one being (in contrast to other religions at the time), communicated to him in a vision of an angel, Vohu Mana, who appeared as a giant, many times the size of a man. He went on to have other visions, and identified six important divine beings, later translated by scholars in the following terms: The Archangel of Prosperity, the Archangel of Right, the Archangel of Piety, the Archangel of Immortality, the Archangel of Dominion, and – highest of all – the Archangel of Good Thought. Under their rule, Zoroaster claimed, were a total of 40 less important angels, known as The Adorable Ones. The Adorable Ones ruled over still more angels, called Guardian Angels, each one assigned to an individual human being. The role of the Guardian Angels, as in later religions, was to guide, help, advise and protect their charge throughout his or her life. The Guardian Angel would also act as the person's conscience at times of moral dilemma.

Some of these angels and archangels were male, others female. Each of them was associated with a particular quality, and they were all held to be attributes of 'the Lord of Light', or Ahura Mazda, as Zoroaster called his central deity. Just as 'truth' and 'lie' are opposites, so Zoroaster held 'the Lord of Light' to be opposed by a 'Lord of Darkness'. And corresponding to the Lord of Light's legions of angels were the Lord of Darkness's hosts of evil demons and spirits. These lesser spirits constantly battled against each other, through different stages of existence. Zoroaster believed that in the final stage of existence, the Lord of Light would eventually win.

Zoroaster's Angels

Zoroaster had a very large number of angels in his religion, including the following:
The Amesha Spentas, translated as 'archangels' or 'benificent immortals', the highest beings created by Ahura Mazda, whose names are: Vohu Mano (Good Thought), who presides over cattle; Asha Vahishta (Justice), who presides over fire; KhshathraVairya (Dominion), who presides over metals; Spenta Armaiti (Devotion), who presides over the earth; Haurvatat (Health), who presides over water; Ameretat (Immortality), who also presides over the earth.

The Yatazas or 'Adorable Ones': Like the Amesha Spentas, these angels personify abstract ideas and virtues. The Yatazas protect human beings from evil and must be honoured and praised as creations of the Lord of Light, Ahura Mazda. They include: Ahurani, female angels who preside over water; Airyaman, angels of friendship and healing; Akhshti, who personifies peace; Arshtat, personifying justice; Ashi Vanghuhi, translated as 'good blessings'; Asman, angel of the sky; Atar, angel of fire (known as the son of Ahura Mazda); Chista, a female angel who presides over religious wisdom; Daena, another female ruling the inner self, or conscience; Dahma, the angel of benediction; Drvaspa, presiding over cattle; Erethe, the female angel who personifies truth; Geush Urvan, the personification of animal life (literally 'the soul of the cow'); Haoma, the angel of the haoma plant (now known as ephedra, which is used by the contemporary followers of the religion, the Parsis, for its medicinal properties); Haptoiringa, the angel of Ursa Major, the star; Khwarenah, the angel of Divine Grace and Fortune; Maonghah, the angel of the moon; Manthra Spenta, the embodiment of the Holy Word; Mithra, the angel of light; Nairyosangha, the messenger of Ahura Mazda, who listens to prayer; Paoiryaenis, the angel of the Pleiades star cluster; Parendi, the angel of abundance; Raman, the angel of joy and happiness; Rapithwin, Rashnu, the angel of justice; Rata, the female angel of charity; Sraosha, the angel who guards the soul for three days after death; Tishtrya, the angel of the star Sirius; Ushah, the female angel of the dawn; Vayu, the angel of the wind; Verethraghna, the angel of victory; Zamyat, the angel of the earth; Zantuma, the angel presiding over the tribe.

The Fravishis or 'guardian angels': These angels originally patrolled heaven, but were sent down to guard humans and keep the demon spirits at bay. There are so many of them that they cannot be named individually, but they are often represented as a male human figure with the wings and tail of a bird. The Fravishis act as models for human beings to emulate, and are the angels that each individual will unite with after death.

ANGELS AS PAGAN GODS AND GODDESSES

The prophet Zoroaster was one of the first religious leaders to elevate one god in the pantheon of his times, Ahura Mazda, above the rest. He then went on to demote all the other pagan gods and goddesses of the nature worshippers around him (mainly Aryans, who worshipped spirits known as 'devas'), and made them into angels serving the one God. In this way, he managed to incorporate all the pagan spirits into his new religious belief system.

Zoroastrianism is an early example of how a polytheistic religion (a religion where believers have many gods) is transformed into a monotheistic one (where believers worship one god only). Angels have a central role in the transition from religions where many gods are worshipped (such as animism and Shamanism, which revere many gods or spirits as embodiments of the elements and animals), to religions teaching that there is only one God. Typically, in this process, one God is chosen as the most important, and all the others are relegated to the position of angels serving the one god. Thus, a pantheon of pagan gods, whom people are very attached to, can be incorporated into the new monotheistic religion as angels, or lesser spiritual beings, who nevertheless must still be honoured and worshipped, often as individual 'guardian angels' looking after one single human being, community, or aspect of human life.

It could be said that in Judaism, pagan elements of ancient religions still exist in the throngs of angels that form part of the theology. In the same way, Christianity holds elements of pagan religions in its panoply of saints, whose lineage can often be traced back to ancient pre-Christian gods and goddesses. This means that, instead of viewing ancient polytheistic cults as primitive forms of worship that have been completely outmoded and superseded by the major world religions, we can see that in many cases, they continue to be part of them. In Judaism, Christianity, and Islam, the ancient gods and goddesses of antiquity often appear in their modern guise, whether as angels and saints – or conversely, as demons and devils.

Ancient Egyptian bas-relief of Ahura Mazda as a winged disk.

THE SEMITIC ANGELS

The early Semitic tribes of the Middle East were animistic in their beliefs – meaning they believed in many spirits of nature, like many other peoples in different parts of the world. They were also influenced by Zoroastrianism, which elevated some of the nature spirits above others, making them into angels serving one God. Among these were the spirits of fire and of wind, which were considered especially significant.

As the Semitic tribes developed a religion centering on one God, known today as Judaism, these spirits were transformed into angels serving God. Over time, they were carefully ranked in importance by Jewish prophets, mystics, and scholars. They also grew in number, following the example of Zoroaster.

The Jewish Angelic Hierarchy

Moses Maimonides was a medieval Jewish philosopher and scholar of the Torah (the five books of Moses, which form the basis of the Jewish faith). Known as 'the great eagle', he classified the angels of the Bible, in order of importance, as follows.

The Chayot

First were what he called the Chayot or 'living beings'. These Chayot each have four wings and four faces. Their faces are those of a man, a lion, an ox, and an eagle. Later, these symbols became signs of the zodiac: Aquarius (the man), Leo (the lion), Taurus (the ox), and Scorpio (the eagle). According to the vision reported in the *Book of Ezekiel*, these angels formed a spectacular battle chariot, known as the Merkabah, driven by a God in the shape of a man. The angels moved quickly, in flashes of light, and beside each one was a wheel with rims that were covered in eyes. Ezekiel reported that God visited him in this way, in a blinding vision of light, and then sent him down to teach the Israelites.

Ezekiel also described the wings of each Chayot. Two were spread across the chariot and connected with the wings of the angels on the other side of it, so that the chariot appeared to be made of wings. The other two wings of the Chayot were used to cover its body. (Later, in Christianity, the chayot were thought to have a different function, which was to hold up the throne of God in heaven, and indeed the earth itself.)

The Ophanim

Nearby the Chayot, Ezekiel recalled, were some other angels who looked like wheels within wheels. These were the Ophanim, who became the second-ranking angels in Maimonides' hierarchy. In the *Book of Enoch*, an ancient Jewish text ascribed to the great-grandfather of Noah, the Ophanim are described as burning in flames, and covered in eyes. Their function is to watch and guard the chariot as it races through the sky. The Ophanim are also mentioned in the Bible, in *Ezekiel* and *Daniel*, where they are sometimes referred to as 'galgallin' or 'thrones', that is, carriers of the throne of God. They are imagined as being always in God's presence, chanting hymns of praise, and are said to mete out divine justice, maintaining cosmic harmony.

The Ophanim appear in many mystic religions, including Rosicrucianism, where they are called 'Lords of the Flame'. They are also often known simply as 'Thrones'. Interestingly, to this day they continue to crop up in popular culture – for example, in the Japanese anime *Digimon Frontier* as the Celestial Digimon called Ophanimon.

The Erelim

Next on Maimonides' list are the Erelim, who are mentioned in the *Book of Isaiah*: 'Behold the Erelim shall cry out, the angels of peace shall weep bitterly'. The name Erelim means 'the valiant' or 'the courageous'. In the Jewish mystic tradition, these angels are connected to moments of sadness, death, and destruction. In various ancient texts, they are described as weeping over Abraham's decision to sacrifice his son Isaac. The Erelim are also said to come down to earth to collect the souls of dead people who have lived a righteous life. Some scholars have drawn a parallel between the Erelim and the Valkyries of Norse mythology, who choose warriors to die in battle and then, once they have fallen, transport them to the Norse heaven, Valhallah.

Strangely, given their propensity to misery and death, the Erelim are also, according to some sources, thought to be the force behind the growth of plants and leaves. The Erelim are also described in the Jewish discipline of Kaballah, and in Christian mysticism.

The Hashmallim

The *Book of Ezekiel* in the Hebrew Bible recounts:

I saw, and behold, there was a stormy wind coming from the north, a great cloud with flashing fire and a brilliance surrounding it; and from the midst of the fire, like the colour of the Hashmal, was the likeness of four Chayot.

The Hashmallim are ranked number four in Maimonides' angel chart. They reappear in the Christian hierarchy of angels, but we know little more about them. However, they reappear in contemporary culture as Hashmal, the leonine beast in the Final Fantasy series of video games set in the world of Ivalice.

The Seraphim

Ranking fifth in Maimonides' angel hierarchy are the Seraphim, who are much better known in Christian theology than other angels. Probably deriving from the ancient animist belief in a spirit of fire, the Seraphim are described as 'the burning ones' in the *Book of Isaiah*. In other parts of the Bible, notably *Numbers* and *Deuteronomy*, they are said to be serpents, possibly because of the connotation of burning pain with the serpent's poisonous bite.

In his vision of the Seraphim in the Temple of Jerusalem, Isaiah sees God sitting up high on a throne, with a long train that fills the temple. Above the throne are a choir of Seraphim, male angels, each of them with six wings: 'with two he covered his face, and with two he covered his feet; and with two he flew'. Isaiah reports that the Seraphim cry out: 'Holy, holy holy, Lord God of Hosts; heaven and earth are full of thy glory.'

Seraphim are also mentioned in the ancient Judaic text, the *Book of Enoch*. Here they are seen as serpents, and stand next to God's throne. They then reappear in the *Book of Revelation*, where they ceaselessly praise the Lord. In the Christian Gnostic text *On the Origin of the World*, which is related to the belief in Yahweh, the Old Testament God, the celestial beings take the form of dragon-shaped angels, thus uniting the two descriptions of the Seraphim as angels and serpents.

These descriptions continue, to this day, to be part of some Jewish religious ceremonies, where the details of Isaiah's vision are repeated in prayers. Literal belief in angels is not always required, however, in modern strands of Judaism. The Seraphim also take on an important role in Christianity, where they are elevated to the first rank of angels surrounding God's throne.

The Malakhim

In modern Hebrew, the word 'mal'akh' means 'angel'. Its roots go back to the Hebrew Bible, which reports that the angels called Malakhim, who were messengers or envoys, appeared to Moses, Joshua, Hagar, Lot, and Abraham, among others. In *Genesis*, they are described as climbing up and down Jacob's Ladder, to heaven; they also feature in many other Bible stories. Isaiah speaks of the Malakhim comforting individuals in their distress, bringing God's presence to them in their affliction; while, the *Book of Psalms* promises that the Malakhim will protect God's people throughout their lives.

The Elohim and Bene Elohim

There is a great deal of dispute about who or what the Elohim (God) and the Bene Elohim (Sons of God) are. Some believe them to be angels, others to be the person of God himself. In the Hebrew Bible, the word is often used as a plural form of 'God', but it is also sometimes used to mean a group of divine beings. Many scholars believe that the ambiguity of this term has to do with the development of a polytheistic religion which has many gods into a monotheistic belief system with only one God at its head. The Bene Elohim, also known as The Watchers, are equally mysterious, and continue to be the subject of much discussion (see page 99).

The Cherubim

In modern times, the Cherubim are often confused with 'cherubs' or baby angels, but in fact, they have nothing to do with them (baby angels, or 'putti', as they are properly called, are fanciful images of infants or toddlers with wings, often found in Renaissance or baroque art). The true Cherubim, who come close to the bottom in the Jewish angelic hierarchy, are mentioned in the Old Testament, and are said to be angels with

Seraphim Purifying the Lips of Isaiah, Catalan School, *c.*15th century.

four wings and four faces. Like the Seraphim, their faces are of a lion, an ox, an eagle or vulture, and a man. Two of their wings are used to hold up God's throne, while two are used to cover their bodies. They have the body and hands of a man, but the feet of a calf.

It is thought that the idea of the Cherubim has its roots in early worship of the bull, or 'shedu' who was often represented with wings and a human head. In ancient times, the 'shedu' was often found in pairs as a statue guarding doorways. Phoenician artists also depicted another winged creature, the Lammasu, a lion with wings and a human head, similar to the Sphinx. Some scholars believe that the Cherubim, and our modern concept of the angel, was derived from the Lammasu.

In keeping with beliefs about the Shedu, early Semitic tribes thought of the Cherubim as guardians who represented the gods and kept trouble away from sacred places. It is also possible that the Cherubim, like the Shedu, were originally storm or wind deities. Several biblical passages describe the Cherubim as 'the wings of the wind'.

The Cherubim play an important role in Jewish mysticism – particularly in the Zohar, the prime work of Kaballah, which states that an angel called Kerubiel is their leader – and later, in Christianity, where they were ranked much higher in the hierarchy of angels (as second only to the Seraphim).

The Ishim

The lowest order of angels, the Ishim, are reported in the *Book of Daniel* to be 'man-like'. However, in other mystical Jewish texts, they are conceived of as being made of snow and fire. The Kaballah cites them as 'the beautiful souls of just men'. In all instances, their function is to continually praise the Lord, like the other angels.

Angel Worship?

Interestingly, considering the effort Maimonides devoted to cataloguing his angels, he did not expect his followers to believe in them literally. He seems to have believed that the angels were created by God to embody his message to humanity. They were endowed with the power of governing nature, and possessed free will; however, they were not like actual humans in that they did not have bodily functions such as needing to eat and sleep.

In his *Guide for the Perplexed*, Maimonides says, 'When man sleeps, his soul speaks to the angel, and the angel to the cherub,' implying that angels take on human form to present revelations to mankind in a way that it can understand, rather than being actual physical entities. In observance of this, the Jewish Bible absolutely forbids the worship of angels.

The 'Sephirot' of Kaballah

Kaballah is a mystical school of thought linked to Judaism. Using Jewish scripture, it seeks to understand the meaning of our universe and the place of humanity within it. The Kabbalists' view of God is a highly conceptual one, in which divine beings, or angels, are seen as 'sephirot', or 'emanations of God' – spiritual powers – which are used to send messages from the heavenly world.

According to the Kaballah, there are ten archangels, each corresponding to a 'sephirot', or attribute of God, and each commanding its own choir. Below these, angels are divided into the following categories: Living Ones, Wheels, Thrones, Brilliant Ones, Fiery Serpents, Messengers, Sons of Godly Beings, Strong Ones, and Souls of Fire. As in mainstream Judaism, each group is named Chayot, Ophanim, Seraphim, and Ishim.

Each of the angels has its own role. Angels in general are known as 'Omdin', or 'Standers', as opposed to human beings, who are called 'Holchim', or 'Walkers'. These names come from the notion that angels always stay the same, and cannot change their natures, whereas human beings change, and can move along a chosen path in life.

Good and Bad Angels

Kabbalah scholars and mystics explain that angels are created by what we humans say and do, either for better or for worse. These angels connect us to a certain frequency. Some frequencies are positive, while others may be negative. Some of the Kaballah teachers claim that each person has two angels who escort him through life, one on the right, and one on the left. The righteous person will honour the angel on the right, while the evil person will always turn to the left.

According to the Kaballah, each time we call on an angel, we invite a certain kind of energy to connect with us. We need to be careful, when doing so, that the energy we call on will be positive, and that we can contain the energy they send. The four essences of life are water, fire, air, and earth. Corresponding to these come the four angels, Michael, Gabriel, Uriel, and Raphael. There are also angels of grace, healing, justice, love, mercy, moon, mountains, paradise, peace, praise, stars, trees, truth, and water, as well as angels of confusion, destruction, fear, fire, hail, insomnia, reptiles, storms, terror, and thunder. Lilith, also called Liliel, is named as the chief she-devil, while Sandalphon is the angel of prayer.

Modern Kaballah

The Kaballah teaches that angels were created before the earth was made. When God said, 'Let there be light', angels came into being. These angels were used as models creation of humanity, and later became jealous of one aspect of the human being's power – free will. Thus, some of them are negative forces, who must be treated with caution.

Today, the Kaballah is experiencing a revival, and has been taken up as a spiritual doctrine by many people, including pop and film celebrities such as Madonna, Demi Moore, and model Naomi Campbell. Madonna's championing of the Kaballah included spending millions of dollars on teaching centres, much to the horror of more traditional followers of the sect. The traditionalists believe that Kaballah cannot, and should not, be separated from the core beliefs of Judaism and promoted worldwide, as rabbis such as Madonna's spiritual guru, Philip Berg, have done, but should be kept as a secret and mystical sect for the faithful few.

Today, the followers of Kaballah in its popular form wear a red string around their wrists to ward off 'the evil eye' and drink blessed water, which costs around £4 a bottle. Rabbi Philip Berg, his wife Karen, and sons Yehuda and Michael, preside over around 60 centres worldwide, offering help to people seeking wealth, health, and happiness.

Greek Mythology

The notion of angels is very much a part of Greek mythology, and influences a great deal of later religious doctrines. The word 'daemon', in its original Greek sense, means a guardian divine being, or an accompanying spirit. In the Greek pantheon of gods, there are a number who can fly, such as Hermes, the winged messenger. Hermes is often pictured with wings on his feet.

The Goddess Nike

Another winged member of the pantheon is the goddess Nike, whose name means 'victory' in Greek. Nike is often seen as a charioteer, riding round the battlefield and choosing victorious ones to reward with glory and fame. The goddess of speed, strength, and victory, Nike was often connected with the goddess Athena, and

was often portrayed on Greek coins. In modern times, she has given her name to the shoe and sports equipment company, Nike.

The idea of human flight also comes into Greek mythology with the tale of Icarus, the man whose father fashioned wings of feathers and wax for him, telling him not to fly too close to the sun. Icarus ignored his instructions, so that the wax in his wings melted, and he fell to his death. This story serves humanity as a reminder not to be too ambitious and try to act like gods, or divine beings.

The Halo of the Angel

Another aspect of Greek mythology that touches on the history of angels is that of the halo. In Greek art, the sun god Helios was often shown with a halo around his head, that is, a circle of light. Over time, in Christian art, expressing the spiritual character of a human figure, whether

angel or saint, came to be done through this symbolism of light, with the halo around the head. In Roman times, emperors who thought highly of themselves often commissioned artists to depict them with a halo around their heads. The halo also appears in Indian Buddhist art from the 3rd century AD, and may have been brought to the east by early Greek invaders.

THE CHRISTIAN ANGEL

The Christian angel is largely based on ideas about angels found in Judaism. However, Christian thinkers also came up with their own concept of the angel, based on their new understanding of, and teaching about, the scriptures. One such thinker was Thomas Aquinas, who in 1259 AD gave a series of lectures about angels at the University of Paris.

Ancient Roman stone carving of the Goddess Nike.

Angels as Pure Intellect

In Aquinas' view, angels represent the ultimate in what might be possible for human nature and intelligence. According to him, angels are first and foremost intellectual beings, who mirror the perfection of God and the universe. They have no bodily form, but are purely composed of spiritual matter. They are not the souls of dead human beings, and are not connected in any way to the body. However, despite this, they sometimes assume the form of human beings, to be able to communicate with us in the physical world.

Aquinas goes on to explain that, even when angels are seen in their bodily form, they are not actually real, live beings. They do not eat, or drink, or have sex, or gain pleasure from the senses, in the way that ordinary mortals do. Their sole reason for taking a bodily form is to communicate to humanity and converse with individual human beings, face to face, so that they can 'give evidence of that intellectual companionship which men expect to have with them in the life to come'. The purpose of these discussions is to reveal the nature of the divine to each one of us, in this way leading humanity to God.

Although angels are usually kind and good, Aquinas also notes that they may have their dangers. One of the dangers he points out is that humans might be led to worship angels instead of God. He emphasizes that angels are only messengers of God, and that even when they appear in visions, what matters is not the angel, but the message they bring from on high. Throughout Christian theology, there is ongoing discussion as to whether angels are simply part of God, or whether they are beings created by God. There are also opposing views as to whether they are male or female; most theologians see them as resembling male humans, and point out that their names are usually masculine.

Throughout the New Testament, angels appear in connection with the birth of Christ and surrounding events. Angels foretell the birth of John the Baptist, appearing to Zachariah to tell him that he and his wife, despite their old age, will have a child who will lead men to God. The famous passage in the Gospel of St Luke tells the story of how the archangel Gabriel appears to the Virgin Mary, telling her that God has chosen her to be the mother of his son, Jesus. Later, angels appear to the shepherds to tell them of the birth of Jesus in a stable. Luke also speaks of an angel comforting Jesus when he waits to be captured, after the Last Supper. At this time, Jesus is in a state of mental torment, having to accept that God wishes him to be sacrificed. According to the Gospel of St Matthew, angels roll back the stone of Jesus' tomb, and an angel also appears after the Resurrection.

In medieval times, scholars and mystics of the Christian faith took the notion of the 'fallen angel' and developed it, using the cosmogony of angels to represent the Seven Deadly Sins. Lucifer, the leader of the fallen angels, was said to represent pride; Mammon to represent avarice; Asmodeus lechery; Satan (in some accounts, a separate being from Lucifer), the sin of anger; Beelzebub gluttony; Leviathan envy; and Belphegor sloth.

Islamic Angels

Certain angels appear both in Judaic and Islamic religious traditions: for example, Michael (Mikail), Gabriel (Jibril) and Raphael (Israfil). In addition, sacred Islamic texts mention several others, including: Azrael, the angel of death, Raqib, who writes good doings, Aatid, who writes bad doings, Maalik, the guardian of hell, and Ridwan, the guardian of paradise.

The angel Jibril plays a very important role in Islamic religion as the messenger who brings Muhammad the first revelation of the Qur'an. Jibril visits Muhammad again when he is sitting outside his house wearing a shroud, once again revealing to him the word of Allah. In another appearance, Jibril takes Muhammad on a long night journey, mounting him on a magical winged creature named Buraq. They fly to Jerusalem, and from there, the angel takes him through the seven heavens. He visits hell and ends his journey in paradise, where he is left alone in the presence of God.

The Jinn or Genie

The Qur'an also mentions another kind of supernatural being that is distinct from the angel. This the jinn, or genie, who occupies a parallel world of ether that exists between our world and heaven. According to Arab folkore, and mentioned in Islamic texts, the jinn are one of the three beings created by Allah; the others are the humans and the angels. The Qur'an says that the jinn are made of a smokeless flame, or the fire of a scorching wind, echoing the primitive spirits of fire and wind mentioned in Shamanism. The jinn are able to change their shape, and as with humans, can be kind and good, or evil and malevolent. Some of them are endowed with free will, like human beings, and a legend is told that when Muhammad preached in the desert, some jinn came to listen to his teachings.

The 'Devil Angel' Iblis

Islamic tradition also records the existence of Shaytan, a word that means 'adversary' or 'opponent', and is connected with the name Satan or Iblis. In the Islamic story, when Allah commanded the angels to bow down to man, the angel Iblis rebelled. As a punishment, he was expelled from heaven. He landed in the mouth of a serpent, and in this way, led Adam and Eve, the first humans, to sin. To this day, he continually tempts men to do evil. On the day of judgement, Iblis will have to account for his actions, and will be thrown into hell.

The chief of the evil spirits is known as al-Shaytan. Al-Shaytan tried to tempt Abraham not to sacrifice his son as Allah had commanded, and for this reason was stoned three times. In memory of this, people throw stones at the pillars at Mina, on the pilgrimage to Mecca.

The Hamalat al'Arsh

The articles of faith in Islam require belief in Allah, his angels, his books, his messengers, the day of judgement, and the idea of predestination, whether good or evil. In Islam, the angels are not ranked in the same way as in Judaism or Christianity. However, some are considered more important than others, usually because of the tasks they carry out. Jibril, or Gabriel, is seen as extremely significant, because it is he who imparts the word of Allah to the prophets, in particular, the Qur'an to Muhammad.

There are many angels who are recognized in Islam, including the Hamalat al'Arsh, who carry the throne of God. Jibril, the angel of Revelation, is also a very high-ranking angel. Then there is Israfil (Raphael), who blows the trumpet at the end of time, as in Judeo-Christian scripture. According to the Qur'an, when Israfil first blows the trumpet, everything on earth will be destroyed; at the second blow, all human beings will come back to life so that they can meet Allah.

Mikail (Michael) is an Islamic angel whose chief role, rather than being a soldier, is to provide help for human beings, bringing food for the body and mind. He is seen as merciful, and brings rewards to those who have led a just life. He is also responsible for bringing rain and thunder to earth.

Azrail, Angel of Death

In Islamic theology, in Sikhism, and some early Hebrew texts, Azrail (in English, Azrael) is named as the angel of death. The Qur'an uses another name for this angel, Malak al-Maut. Azrail means 'whom God helps'.

Azrail takes many forms, some of them evil (as in Jewish mysticism), and some of them good. Physically, he mutates, for example, having four faces and four thousand wings, with a body that consists wholly of eyes and tongues. The number of eyes and tongues is exactly the same as the number of people on earth. Azrail has the job of recording the names of babies born, and of rubbing the names out when each person dies. In some cultures, such as the Berber tribe of Morocco, men shave their heads, leaving a lock of hair in the middle, so that Azrail can pull them up to heaven when they die.

The Seven Heavens

According to Islam, there are seven heavens. The angels who reside in them are Hafaza, or guardian angels, some of whom are called Kiraman Katibin, or Honourable Recorders. Each human being has two of these angels, Raqib, who writes down good deeds, and Aatid, who writes down bad ones. The Hafaza also include Mu'aqqibat, or Protectors, who keep people safe from death until their predestined time comes, and who call down blessings. The angels Nakir and Munkar have the job of questioning dead souls in their graves, while Darda'il, the Journey angels, travel far and wide, looking for places where people are gathered to worship Allah. Finally, there are a number of unknown angels whose task it is to look after each creature on earth, warding off evil and keeping order in the world.

Zabaniah, Angels of Hell

Outside heaven, there are more angels. Maalik is the chief of the angels who rule Hell, governing 19 angels known as Zabaniah, who spend their time torturing unfortunate sinners in the afterlife. The angel Ridwan is the one who guards the gate of paradise. The size and number of angels' wings plays an important part in Islamic descriptions. Jibril is said to have 400 wings, and to have wings so large that if he opened one of them, it would cover the whole world, east to west. Moreover, as mentioned above, some angels, such as Jibril and Mikail, are said to have thousands of wings. In the Islamic faith, it is believed that animals, babies, and children can sometimes see angels. This is, in some cases, because there was an angel present when the babies were born; the angel may, afterwards, continue to swing the cot in which they lie.

Scene still from *Hellboy II: The Golden Army*, directed by Guillermo Del Toro, 2008.

St. Michael, Byzantine School, *c.*14th century.

THE ARCHANGELS

THE ARCHANGEL MICHAEL

The Archangel Michael is one of the most important angels in the Jewish, Christian, and Islamic religions. Michael is envisaged in these traditions as a warrior hero, the leader of God's Army. The name Michael, in Hebrew, means, 'god-like', and has come to be seen as the patron saint of soldiers. In some belief systems, he is seen as the embodiment of Christ before his descent to earth to become man; in others, as the divine spirit of Adam, the first man, in the story of Genesis.

Michael is also mentioned in the Bible as a prince whose particular responsibility, apart from fighting in the cause of God, is to protect, support, and guide children. In the east, he was seen as a healer, and in the west as a patron of war. During the medieval period, he was represented by Christians as the patron saint of chivalry, alongside St George. In this role, he became central to early chivalric orders, such as the Order of St Michael in 1469 in France. Since that time, he has lent his name as patron saint of many societies and organizations.

Michael the Protector

In the *Book of Enoch*, an ancient Judaic text dating from the 1st century BC which greatly influenced both Jewish and Christian religious teachers for many centuries afterwards, there is a description of the archangel Michael as 'the prince of Israel'. Here, he shows another aspect, as kind and compassionate. While he is seen as fierce and noble in war, he is also admired for his qualities of mercy, patience, and fairness. In the Jewish tradition, Michael often intervenes to help one of the founding fathers of the religion, for instance, saving Abraham from being burned to death in a furnace by the warrior Nimrod, and rescuing Lot when the city of Sodom is destroyed. Michael also protects women such as Sarah, Abraham's wife, from harm, and on numerous occasions saves Jacob, another patriarch, from harm. Some believe that, in

the story where Jacob wrestles with the angel, it is Michael whom he pits himself against, and who afterwards forgives him. Michael is also said to be the mentor of Moses, and the divine being who speaks to Moses when he sees the burning bush. Many tales are told in which Michael protects the first human being on earth, Adam, continuing to guard Adam even after he and Eve are banished from the garden of Eden. Significantly, Moses is said to bow down before humanity, and remains the only angel in heaven to do so.

The Christian Michael

The archangel Michael plays an important role in the Christian tradition, as a warrior against Satan. He is often depicted treading on a serpent, carrying the scales of justice as well as his battle sword. In the *Book of Jude*, he is described as fighting in the war in heaven, against a great dragon symbolizing Satan. As in the Jewish religion, Michael is seen by Christians as a warrior and protector; however, the early Christians also made a number of saints, such as St George and St Demetrius, their patrons of war. Michael sometimes appears as a helper to the sick and infirm, emphasizing his kind and caring role. In various legends, Michael causes a magical spring to spout out of the ground; those who bathe there are cured of their illnesses.

Appearances of Michael

Many tales are told of Michael appearing to people on earth with tidings from heaven. In one legend known as the Miracle of Chonae, Michael appears to protect a church that was going to be flooded, splitting a rock to direct the river away from it. In another, he appeared to fishermen at St Michael's Mount, Cornwall. In 1751, a Portuguese Carmelite nun, Antonia d'Astonaco, reported that Michael had appeared to her and asked her to make some special prayers to him; these prayers later found their way into

the liturgy of Catholic church. Other revelations include the visions of some schoolgirls in a village called San Sebastian de Garabandel in Cantabria, northern Spain, between 1961 and 1965.

In another instance, a boy of 13 was said to come out in cuts and scratches whenever the name of St Michael was mentioned. The boy would see a vision of St Michael fighting with the Devil and 10 demons. The boy would then cry out in the voice of St Michael. These visions were reported by Father Raymond Bishop, a Jesuit priest at St Louis University, and used by the author of the novel *The Exorcist*, William Peter Blatty.

Many places have been designated as shrines to Michael, who is viewed as a saint as well as an archangel in the Christian tradition. These include the Mont St Michel in Normandy, France, and the Golden Domed Monastry of St Michael in Kiev, Ukraine.

Michael among Jehovah's Witnesses

Among Jehovah's Witnesses, the archangel Michael is seen as the Son of God, or Jesus, before he came to earth, and also afterwards, when he ascended to heaven. The idea in the Bible that Michael was 'god-like' is evidence for this belief, since as God's son, Michael would be similar to his father in heaven. This connection between Michael and Jesus as one and the same being is also found among Seventh Day Adventists, who believe that Jesus, before he came to earth was the archangel Michael. Michael, according to them, is the 'word of God', rather than a created being, who later descended to earth and was born as Mary's son, Jesus.

Islamic Mikail

Michael also takes an important place in the Islamic faith, and is known as Mikail. Although Mikail is only mentioned once in the Qur'an, he makes many appearances is the Prophet's Hadith (stories about the words and deeds of the prophet Muhammed). In one of these, Muhammed is told by the angel Jibril (Gabriel) that Mikail rules the world of plants and rain. In another, the story is told that Mikail has never laughed since fire was created. Muhammed is also said to pray to God to bless Mikail, along with the angels Jibril and Rafail (Raphael).

Michael in the Occult

Michael figures in the Theosophist movement, which gained followers in the 19th century. This doctrine taught that all religions are attempts to evolve humanity to a greater degree of perfection, and that there is a grain of truth in all of them. There is also a strong element of mysticism in the movement, which was established by Helena Blavatsky and others in New York. According to the theosophist Louis Claude de St Martin, St Michael finally finished his battle with the dragon in 1879. This was reiterated by the philosopher and educationalist Rudolf Steiner, who founded the movement known as anthroposophy, which attempted to investigate spiritual experiences through cultivating the imagination and our intuitive faculties in a creative way.

THE ARCHANGEL GABRIEL

The archangel Gabriel is one of the most popular and well-known of the heavenly angels, whose main function is to deliver messages from God to mortal beings on earth. In his most famous role, he appears to the Virgin Mary and tells her that God has chosen her to be the mother of the Son of God. There are many paintings of this pivotal moment in the Christian faith, which is commonly called The Annunciation. Gabriel is also the angel who foretells the birth of John the Baptist. The Bible describes him as looking like a very beautiful mortal man, but over time, some retellings of the story, especially in different forms of mysticism, have made him female or of indeterminate sex.

Similarly, Gabriel has a central role to play in the Islamic religion, appearing to the prophet Muhammed and revealing the holy text of the Qur'an to him. In the Muslim faith, Gabriel is the most important of all the angels, known as the Holy Spirit (Islam) who speaks to Muhammed.

Gabriel the Messenger

There are many mentions of the angel Gabriel in the Bible. The prophet Daniel tells of Gabriel as a man-like angel who visits him to impart knowledge and understanding of his visions. In other instances, Gabriel, who is called a 'chief prince', prophesies important events. Some strands of Judaism describe Gabriel as standing at the Throne of Glory in heaven, at the left hand side of God. There are three other angels who also stand at the throne, including Michael. In keeping with his role as messenger, Gabriel is seen, in the Christian and Islamic religions, as the angel of revelation. In Jewish mysticism, he is also described as the angel of fire, and is associated with the colour red. In many instances, he is seen as the angel of death, in particular, appearing at the point of death of kings and princes. Gabriel is sometimes mentioned as working in tandem with Michael, and, like Michael, may sometimes play the role of protector and guardian to the weak and defenceless.

The New Testament tells the story of how Gabriel appeared to the parents of John the Baptist, Zacharias and Elizabeth, telling them that they would have a son who would be a great prophet. In the story, Gabriel brings out a horn and announces himself by name. Gabriel makes another appearance when he visits Mary, a relative of Elizabeth's, and tells her:

Do not fear, Mary, for you have found favour with God. And behold! You shall conceive in your womb and bear a son, and you shall call his name Jesus… The Holy Spirit shall come

on you, and the power of the Highest shall overshadow you. Therefore also that Holy One which will be born of you shall be called the Son of God. And behold, your cousin Elizabeth also conceived a son in her old age. And this is the sixth month with her who was called barren. For with God nothing shall be impossible.

Gabriel's Trumpet

Possibly because of the association with his horn, mentioned in the New Testament, Gabriel is often seen as the angel who blows the last trumpet on Judgement Day, marking the end of time, although there is no actual mention of this in the Bible. It is thought that the idea might originate in Norse mythology, where the guardian of the bridge between heaven and earth, Heimdall, blows a great horn to announce Ragnarok, the start of an epic battle that will cause death and destruction but will eventually lead to the dawning of a new era.

In mathematics, Gabriel's horn, also called Torricelli's trumpet, is a geometric figure having an infinite surface area but enclosing a finite volume. The Italian physicist and mathematician Evangelista Torricelli, first studied the properties of this figure, whose shape resembles a trumpet. In some Christian traditions, just as Michael is said to appear on earth as Jesus or Adam, Gabriel is said to be the divine being who comes down to earth as the patriarch Noah. This view is taken in the Church of the Latter-Day Saints, which is a Christian sect linked to the Mormon faith.

The Muslim Jibril

In the Muslim religion, Gabriel, or Jibril, appears as the angel who gives the prophet Muhammed the holy Qur'an. In the Hadith, a collection of stories explaining the meaning of Muhammed's teachings, Jibril is described as having six hundred wings, each of which cover the horizon. The wings are said to scatter jewels, pearls, and rubies. The Qur'an also recounts how Gabriel appeared to the Virgin Mary, foretelling the birth of Jesus – although in the Qur'an, Jesus is seen as a prophet, rather than the Son of God. The Qur'an retains the mystery of Jesus being born to a virgin, explaining it as occurring through the will of Allah. Other stories in the Qur'an narrate how Gabriel accompanies Muhammed when he ascends to heaven. Gabriel is also said to descend to earth on 'The Night of Destiny', which is the night when the Qur'an is thought to have been first revealed, and which is celebrated in the holy month of Ramadan.

THE ARCHANGEL RAPHAEL

In Hebrew, the name Raphael means 'God Heals', and many stories within the Judaic, Christian, and Islamic traditions tell of this angel's power to heal the sick. The name is also linked to the Hebrew word 'Rophe', meaning medical doctor. Raphael is often pictured holding a bottle or phial, which symbolizes his ability to bring relief to those suffering from illness.

In the *Book of Tobit*, which is considered as scripture by some branches of Christianity and not others, the angel Raphael accompanies the character of Tobias, the son of devout parents who are suffering greatly. The father, Tobias is blind, while the mother is plagued by a demon prince, Asmodeus, who has killed her former husbands. Tobias needs to make a long journey to get help for them, so Raphael disguises himself as a human being, Azarias, and comes down to accompany him on the journey. In one episode of the story, Raphael catches a large fish, later using magical parts of it to heal Tobit's blindness and to drive Asmodeus away from his mother. The story eventually ends happily, as Tobias brings aid to his virtuous parents. The moral of the story is that the just and devout will be rewarded; that God is good and kind. Suffering is seen as a test of faith, rather than as a punishment. In the book,

Stained glass window depicting the Angel Gabriel, *c.*20th century.

we are told that Raphael is one angel 'of seven that stand before the Lord', but we are not told who the others are.

Largely because of this story, Raphael has come to be the patron saint of medical workers, travellers, the sick, and others in need. Another story in the New Testament tells of an angel who comes to alight on a pond where sick people were being bathed. When the water moved, the sick people recovered from their illnesses. This angel is generally taken to be Raphael, though he is not mentioned by name.

As well as being pictured holding the bottle or phial, Raphael is sometimes represented as carrying a fish, because of the story mentioned above. In other paintings, he carries a staff and walks alongside Tobias. Raphael's kindness in descend-ing to earth in human form as a companion for the young Tobias has given him a special place in religious traditions of all kinds as a guardian angel, especially of young people, travellers, and the sick.

The Islamic Israfil

In the Hadith, Israfil or Raphael, rather than Gabriel, is mentioned as the angel who blows the horn at Judgement Day. The horn is described as emitting a 'blast of truth'. The first blast signals the beginning of Judgement Day, and the second summons the souls of all people to gather together, somewhere in a place between heaven and hell, to be judged for their conduct during their lives.

Ceiling decoration in the Hagia Sophia, featuring archangel Uriel.

THE ARCHANGEL URIEL

Uriel is a rather mysterious archangel whose name is linked in various occult works with Jacob, Raphael, and others. He does not appear in the mainstream holy texts of any religion, but is mentioned quite often in what is called 'apocryphal' scripture – that is, stories that are not generally held to be of divine inspiration by the established church. For example, he appears in some ancient religious stories (for example, mystic writings called Gnostic gospels) under the name Uriel or Phanuel as 'the light of God'. In the *Book of Esdras*, another ancient work, Uriel instructs the prophet Ezra in the meaning of God's teaching. Esdras names several angels, including Michael, Gabriel, Raphael, and Uriel, as the ones who will rule the world at the end of time. In addition, he names other angels such as Beburos, Zebuleon, and Aker, who are not found anywhere else in the religious texts.

Uriel also appears in the Christian apocrypha as the rescuer of John the Baptist from Herod's massacring armies. He also helps John the Baptist and John's mother Elizabeth to join Jesus, Mary, and Joseph after they have fled to Egypt. Uriel is pictured in Leonardo da Vinci's famous *Virgin of the Rocks*, sitting to the left of Mary.

Uriel is often depicted as carrying a scroll or book, representing wisdom. However, in other incarnations, he acts as a fierce, somewhat terrifying angel carrying a fiery sword. He is sometimes identified as the 'flame of God', and in some stories is known as 'the angel of repentance', presiding over sinners on Judgement Day.

THE 'WATCHERS'

One of the strangest groups of angels are the Watchers, also known as Grigori. These angels are described in the apocryphal *Book of Enoch*. The Watchers are fallen angels who have mated with human women, giving rise to a hybrid race known as the Nephilim. In the *Book of Enoch*, the Watchers are said to number 200.

The leader of the Watchers is an angel called Samyaza, whose name means 'infinite rebellion'. In a rather lurid passage, Samyaza and his group of angels, who are initially dispatched to earth to watch over human beings, begin to lust for women. They have sex with the women, and a race of giant mutants is born – the Nephilim.

The Nephilim

Unlike the story of the Watchers, that of their descendents, the Nephilim, occurs in the Bible, in *Genesis* and *Numbers*. They are also mentioned in several other religious texts. In the Bible, the Nephilim are mentioned as 'giants' who are so huge that human beings seem like grasshoppers in comparison. These giants have savage ways, and Samyaza instructs them in the black arts and the art of war. They have knowledge of techniques that will bring destruction upon the earth. They are evil beings, who tried to lead ordinary mortals astray through idolatry and the black arts. It is suggested, in the *Book of Jubilees*, that God sent the great flood to rid the earth of the Nephilim, but that some of them still survived afterwards, and continue to exert a demonic influence over humans whenever they get the chance.

In some interpretations of these early texts, the Nephilim are the descendents of Seth, the third son of Adam and Eve, and brother to Cain and Abel. These descendents marry into the lineage of Cain, whose people do not worship God. When the new race began to behave badly, wreaking havoc with their evil ways, God was moved to get rid of them by ordering the flood.

BUDDHIST AND HINDU ANGELS

THE BUDDHIST 'DEVA'

In the Buddhist religion, a deva, devata, or devaputra is a spiritual being who may resemble a human, but is superior in many ways. Devas are not visible to the human eye, but may be seen or heard by human beings who have a special extrasensory power known as a 'divyacakus'. This power enables them to detect beings from another plane of existence, such as the deva.

Like angels, devas take on a bodily form so that they can show themselves to us on the human plane of existence. Devas from different planes of existence have to show themselves to each other in this way. Buddhists believe that there are 31 planes, or states of existence, in the universe, only one of which is the human plane that we know. Beings are born on different planes according to how much 'karma' they have accumulated as a result of good thoughts and deeds. Above the human planes are the 'deva' and 'brahma' planes.

The 'Deva' Plane

Life in the 'deva' plane is different from that on earth. It is a subtle plane of existence where the deva enjoys great sensual pleasure, long life, and contentment, as well as the ability to use their supernatural powers. The 'brahma' plane is said to be a place of formless beings, who have no material bodies. These beings transcend physical sensation and exist in a state of balance. The beings on the 'brahma' plane are described as celestial, and correspond to the 'gods' of Western religious traditions.

The Lower Planes

Below the human plane of existence are four planes, known as 'asura', 'peta', 'thiracchana', and 'niraya'. These are planes where human beings who have not developed much 'karma' in their lives, (for example, by being greedy and materialistic) may end up when they are reborn into a new life. (The Buddhist faith, as is well known, teaches the doctrine of reincarnation.)

In contrast to the Judaic, Christian, and Islamic concepts of heaven and hell, the Buddhist view is that there are many planes of existence, some lower, some higher, than our own. Devas are similar to angels to the degree that 'devas' may appear to us in the human realm, to teach us about ways of life in a higher plane. Also, devas, like angels, may be 'emanations' of benevolent deities, good thoughts, or higher beings, as in Western traditions.

According to Buddhist teaching, the devas on higher spiritual planes than our own do not eat, drink, and sleep, as human beings do; however, the lower-ranking ones may well have the same physical needs as humans. Like angels, the higher devas are illuminated by light, can fly through the air, and are capable of moving at great speed over large territories. They may also use chariots to ride across the sky.

The Hierarchy of Devas

In the Buddhist faith, there is great subtlety and fluidity regarding the nature of spiritual beings and their incarnations, which is often absent from the other great religious traditions. Beings can move between different planes, and manifest themselves in different ways to each other, and in this way are not necessarily fixed in one time or place. Having said that, there is a hierarchy of devas in the Buddhist cosmogony, with the important feature that the devas may shift through the different ranks according to various conditions, such as their accumulation of karma, and so on.

Devas fall into three main groups, according to which 'dhatu', or 'realm' they are born into. Devas born into the 'Arupyadhatu' realm or element have no physical form. They are in a sense pure mind, meditating on formless subjects. They may achieve this through meditating to a higher plane from another existence. These devas do not have anything to do with other realms, and do not influence human action directly.

The Heavens

In the same way, devas born into the realm of 'Rupadhatu' have no physical forms. They are sexless, passionless beings. In this realm, there are many deva worlds, or Heavens, that rise above the earth in a series of layers. Each of these heavens has a different type of deva in it.

Buddhist followers known as 'Angamins' who have died before attaining the highest states of enlightenment known as 'Arhat' may be reborn as 'Suddhavasa' devas. These devas will make it their task to protect and guide Buddhists on earth, somewhat as Christian angels lead mortals to God. Eventually, the devas will pass away into a higher plane, and achieve 'Arhat' in a different form. According to some Buddhist teachings, human beings originally had the powers of the higher devas: that is, their bodies were made of light, they did not need to eat, and they could fly. Over a long period of time, their powers began to fade, they began to eat food, and their bodies became more physical. Male and female genders separated into the 'deva' (the male) and the 'devi' (the female).

Devas and Angels

Although there are many similarities between the concepts of the angel and the deva, there are also some important differences. Buddhist devas are not immortal, as angels are. Although they may live for thousands, or even billions, of years, their lifetime is finite. They move between different planes of existence by being reborn as another type of being, whether another deva, a human, or another creature, known or unknown. In addition, devas come into being as a result of their balance of karma, and do not have a role in governing the world, as many angels from the Judeo-Christian or Islamic religions do. Neither do they have a role in the passing away of one world to another; there is no parallel, for example, of the angel Gabriel sounding the trumpet at Judgement Day in Buddhist thought.

Unlike angels, who embody various traits of God, devas are all separate beings. Like humans, they have their own individual characteristics, moral qualities, and destinies. In the same way as humans, they are not omniscient, or omnipotent; their understanding is partial, and their power limited. They do not intrude on human affairs, and may only intervene to give advice. Moreover, they are not perfect. Although they may possess higher qualities than humans, they may also be limited by pride, ignorance, and arrogance. The devas of the lower realms, rather like demons in Judeo-Christian or Islamic thought, may behave worse than many humans, being lustful, angry, and malevolent.

The Hindu Devas

In the Hindu cosmogony, 'deva' is a general word for deity. Since there are many gods and goddesses in the Hindu pantheon, these 'devas' are sometimes seen as a type of 'angel' or celestial being. Indeed, the word 'deva' means 'the shining one', and is also connected to the word for sky.

The Hindu faith is based on the *Vedas*, early sacred texts originating in India. These texts are written in a form of Sanskrit, and contain mantras or prayers which, through repeating certain sounds or words, are used to uplift the religious seeker, effecting a spiritual transformation. Some of the *Vedas* are mantras to please the devas, so that blessings will come on the supplicants. The *Vedas* also give information about the many devas, which range in the texts, and later additions to it, from dozens to millions.

The Vedic Devas

Like the Semitic, Islamic, and Christian angels, the devas have particular characteristics. They may, in some cases, represent moral values; in others, they are forces of nature. In the *Rigveda*, one of the central Vedic texts, the main devas mentioned are Varuna (god of sky, water, and the underworld), Mitra (god of honesty and friendship) , and Indra (god of war, storms, and rain). Other devas like Savitr (god of fire and vitality), Vishnu (the supreme god, the maintainer and preserver), and Rudra (the god of wind or storm) also appear; in addition, there are 'devis', goddesses such as Ushas (dawn), Prithvi (earth), and Sarasvati (knowledge).

Like most other world religions, some of the spiritual beings described in the Hindu faith have their roots in early nature worship. Thus, the *Vedas* describe the devas as running into millions, 330 million to be exact, all of them reflecting some aspect of nature, such as Agni (fire), Vayu (air) and so on. In the same way, in the Judeo-Christian tradition, early nature gods, such as the god of fire, inspired our concept of angels such as the Seraphim. This process of taking a host of nature spirits from early Shamanistic cultures, and blending them into a hierarchy of angels, celestial beings, and spiritual entities surrounding a central God, seems to be a worldwide phenomenon, and one that happens as much in eastern traditions as in the West.

The Garuda — Winged Being of the East

The Garudua is a bird-like creature that appears in both the Hindu and the Buddhist religious traditions. In the Hindu faith, Garuda is a lesser divinity. He has a golden body, that of a muscular young man, and an eagle's beak. His face is white, his wings are red, and he wears a large crown on his head. He is envisaged as very large, so that when he flies across the sun, the world is plunged into darkness. The sound of his wings beating

Dancing Devatas in The Bayon Temple, Angkor Thom, Cambodia.

is likened, in some texts, to that of the chanting of prayers. In the *Vedas*, Garuda is described as having brought nectar from heaven to earth. In this way, Garuda functions much as an angel, bringing spiritual succour from on high to people on earth below.

The story of Garuda's birth is told in the Mahabharata, one of the great epic legends of India. Garuda is said to have been born from an egg, first appearing as a raging fire large enough to burn up the whole world. He was so terrifying that the gods begged him for mercy. He listened to their prayers and made himself smaller in response. There are many tales of his adventures through life, including that of rescuing his mother from her evil sister, the serpent goddess Kadru. In order to do this, he had to bring the elixir of immortality, which was guarded by the god, to the serpents. After many great battles, he managed to do this, in the process making friends with the gods, and becoming the enemy of snakes. In many pictures of the legend, he is shown with the god Vishnu riding on his back, as well as other gods and goddesses from the Hindu pantheon.

As in Judeo-Christian and Islamic notions of the angel, the Garuda is seen as a protector and avenger to those who pray to him for help. He is typically shown as flying down with great speed to kill a serpent, showing tremendous violence as he does so.

The Buddhist Garuda

Connected to the Hindu Garuda is the Buddhist Garuda or Supara, whose name means 'having good wings'. The Garuda is seen as one of the minor devas of the Buddhist pantheon, because as well as having divine aspects, it is also animal in nature.

The Buddhist Garuda, like the Hindu Garuda, is a large creature with huge wings that create darkness and a wind as strong as a hurricane when it flies. If the Garuda flies over a village or town, the houses may fall down in its wake. It is many times larger than a human being, so much so that a man can hide in its plumage without being noticed. The Garuda is said to be so strong that it is able to tear up a banyan tree from its roots and carry it off in its beak. It also has a magical ability to change its size, growing large or small at will. At its largest, its wing span is over a thousand miles long. If it flaps its wings over the sea, the sea can dry up, and the Garuda will then fly down and eat all the sea creatures, including large dragons, on the dry sea bed. The Garuda can also move mountains by pushing them into the sea with its wings. In addition, the Garuda is also able to adopt human form. In its human form, the Garuda may come down to earth and court a human woman. There are tales of the Garuda romancing women in its dwelling place among the groves of the beautiful silk cotton 'simbali' tree.

The Nagas

Garudas or Suparas have a traditional enemy: the Nagas, a race of dragon-like snakes who are highly intelligent, crafty, and malicious beings. The Garudas spend their time hunting these creatures, killing them by biting off their heads. However, the Nagas, to combat this, have developed the habit of eating large stones, thus making their heads too heavy for the Nagas to carry off. According to legend, the ascetic teacher Karambiya taught the Garuda how to deal with this problem. Prior to biting off the serpent's head, the Garuda must take the Naga by the tail, biting it until the Naga is forced to vomit up the stone.

The Hindu Ahura

Just as the Garuda's natural enemy is the Naga, so the Hindu deva's opposite is the Asura. The Asura are a group of malevolent, power-hungry deities, sometimes described as being evil and greedy. In some ways, they are rather similar to the Judeo-Christian and Islamic concept of the 'fallen angel': divine beings that have sinned against God, and have been cast into a lower realm, where they prey on the weaknesses of human beings, tempting them to immoral acts.

In early Hindu texts, the Asura were not seen in a particularly negative light. As humble devas they were said to preside over the affairs of human beings, governing such areas as marriage and everyday moral issues. In later texts, however, they begin to develop a combative relationship with the higher devas, and eventually are conceived of as the 'evil ones', in contrast to the more benevolent celestial beings. The Bhagavad Gita, an important religious text ascribed to the teaching of Lord Krishna, describes how all beings in the universe take on divine or material qualities. While the devas embody positive qualities, the Asura embody negative ones, such as ignorance, conceit, pride, anger, and arrogance.

Garuda carrier of Lord Vishnu, *c.*19th century.

PAGAN ANGELS: THE VALKYRIES

One of the most striking figures in Norse mythology is the Valkyrie. The name means 'chooser of the slain', and legend has it that when men fight in battle, a host of celestial women called Valkyries fly through the sky in chariots, deciding who will die and who will be saved. The men chosen to die are brought back by the Valkyries to a great hall that serves as their home in the afterlife: Valhalla.

The Valkyrie also have other roles, such as becoming lovers to heroic soldiers. They are sometimes described as being from royal lineage. They are associated in the mythology with such birds as ravens and swans. What we know about them comes from the *Poetic Edda*, a book of 13th-century poems based on traditional lore, and other works from the same period. The *Poetic Edda* mentions many Valkyries, including Skuld (the shield bearer), Skogul (the shaker), Gunnr (the war queen), Hildr (the battle queen), Gondul (the wand bearer), and Geirskogul (the spear carrier).

The Valkyrie Sigrun

One tale concerns Helgi Hundingsbane, a young man who witnesses Valkyries flying through the air to the battlefield. Their clothes are drenched in blood and their spears are shining. However, they protect Helgi. After the battle is over, the Valkyries fly away, but one of them, Sigrun (meaning 'victory rune') stays behind, and eats the corpses, along with the wolves. Sigrun then tells Helgi that he will be a great ruler, and pledges to become his protector. Later, when Helgi eventually dies in battle, Sigrun

Illustration for the opera *Die Valkure*, by Richard Wagner.

is heartbroken and dies from grief. However, according to some sources, there was a belief in reincarnation among the Nordic peoples, and some other accounts tell how Helgi and Sigrun were reborn and reunited after many years of separation.

Brynhildr the Warrior

We also hear of the Valkyrie Brynhildr, who is found in a building on a mountain, wearing a helmet and a coat of mail. When a young man, Sigurd, comes across the building, he stops to have a look at it, finds her, and cuts the mail away from her. This motif, of a woman disguised as a man by wearing a battle helmet and a coat of mail, recurs often in Norse mythology.

Valkyries are believed to converse with birds, especially ravens. In many tales, they are said to be very beautiful, with golden hair, white skin and bright eyes. Although mortal men fall in love with them, they are not as a rule interested in romance, except occasionally with the more heroic figures. This is perhaps because if they lose their virginity, they will no longer be immortal.

There is also a sinister aspect to the Valkyries. In one story, a man looks through the window of a hut, and inside sees the Valkyries weaving on a loom, using the heads of men as weights, and their entrails as the warp and weft of the fabric. A sword is used as a shuttle. As they weave, the Valkyries decide who is to be killed at an upcoming battle. Then, when they have finished the work, they tear down the loom, keeping pieces of it in their hands, mount their horses, and ride off.

Demons of the Dead

Evidently, the Valkyries are ambiguous figures. They have a strong link with death, and a power over mortal men to decide who will die first. It has been suggested that they originated in German paganism, and may have been 'demons of the dead'. There may also have been connections to the female Irish shield warriors, and to the Norns, supernatural women who determine the destiny of each human being.

Many believe that the Valkyries represent a very ancient belief in the spiritual importance of the carrion crow, and that they are a type of early 'corpse goddess', somewhat similar to the Celtic Morrigan (see pp.00-00). Over the centuries, they began to be depicted as more benign creatures, often on small amulets and memorial stones. Here, they appeared as beautiful and welcoming, often with long blond hair and blue eyes, wearing a scarlet corset, and holding a horn of mead, rather than the spears and shields. Later still, they became 'swan maidens', beautiful women with white feathered robes. Legend has it that if the swan maiden can be captured and held, the capturer may make a wish, and it will be granted. That is why the swan maiden is also known as the wish maiden.

The Goddess Freya

There are many conflicting accounts as to the role of the goddess Freya, but certainly in some tales she appears as the leader of the Valkyries. She is the Norse goddess of love, beauty, and fertility, as well as the goddess of battle and death. She travels through the sky on a chariot drawn by great cats, or on a boar with golden bristles. She is able to turn herself into a bird of prey by donning a magic cloak of falcon feathers. She, and the other Valkyries, may sometimes appear before a battle and predict the outcome. When she rides forth, the light in the sky begins to flicker; it is she who causes the famous Northern Lights, or Aurora Borealis, to appear.

CELTIC FAIRIES

The fairy is related to the angel in many ways. Most obviously, in later traditions of fairy lore, fairies are conceived of as supernatural beings with wings that are able to fly (unlike in early fairy tales, where fairies do not have wings but ride around on the backs of insects). Rather like the Christian angel, fairies also have an input into our daily lives, often foreseeing, or influencing, human destiny.

Where the fairy differs from the angel is that the 'little people', as they are often called, are usually mischievous beings, meddling in people's plans for no other reason than to be interfering. In this way, the fairy could be seen as more akin to a Christian demon, or one of the lower Buddhist devas. In some folk tales, there are stories of fairies as a type of fallen angel, thus explaining their malevolent intent.

Enchantment or 'Faerie'

The belief in fairies, a supernatural race of beings with whom we share the planet, has existed for centuries. Among many different cultures around the world, fairy myths and legends abound. They are particularly strong in the British Isles, and widespread in Ireland. In these folk tales, fairies take on different attributes: they may be tiny or gigantic, impossibly beautiful or ugly and misshapen. They may be conceived of as good-natured and charming, or as evil and malicious; as winged creatures who are obviously supernatural, inhabiting an unearthly realm, or as beings who look just like humans and live as neighbours with us. There is a huge range of stories about the 'fairy folk' and their relationship to 'the human kind', but almost all of them have a few features in common.

In most of the stories, fairies, like angels, are seen as having the power to predict and control the fate of human beings. Indeed, the name 'faerie' derives from the Latin term 'fata', meaning fate. Fairies may use this power to help or to hinder those who come into contact with them; but they tend to be mischievous, so they must always be approached with caution.

Fairies also have the power to cast spells and to hold humans in a state of 'fayerie' or enchantment, so that they leave their earthly responsibilities and family ties behind, held by an illusion. This state is akin to falling in love or being in a state of sexual thrall. For this reason, fairies are greatly feared, and in many cultures, there are rituals and customs designed to appease or ward off the fairies so that individuals or families will not be harmed.

The 'Fair Folk'

Fairies also have the power to live unseen or unnoticed among human beings. Thus, when referring to them, humans must take care not to annoy them. In different cultures, they are called a variety of polite names; for example, in Wales, 'the fair folk'; in Scotland, 'the good neighbours'; in Ireland, 'the silent people'. Other names, such as the Nordic ' alfar' (or elves) emphasize their role as spirits of nature: for example, mountain sprites, water sprites, and tree sprites. According to some legends, fairies are the handmaidens or henchmen of powerful monsters and demons, which is an additional reason to be wary of them.

Among the Celtic countries, fairy lore has flourished, and can still be found today in Ireland, Scotland, Wales, Brittany and parts of Germany. In the folklore of these regions, fairies are seen as a race of beings equal to, and possibly more ancient than, humanity, who live underground in hills and among rocks, who move around noiselessly, and who often intrude on the lives of ordinary folk, meddling in their day-to-day lives in such a way that disaster often occurs. For example, fairies might steal a human child and substitute a fairy child or 'changeling' of their own, or kidnap a young man that they have

taken a fancy to, causing him to abandon his wife and children.

The Seelie and Unseelie Court

Fairies are also said to 'pay a tithe to hell', for which they gain the power to enchant human beings. They may, in some stories, be servants of demons, fallen angels, or other evil supernatural beings. In Scots mythology, fairies are said to belong to the Seelie Court (good fairies) or the Unseelie Court (evil fairies).

The activities of the fairies range from effecting irritating practical jokes, such as curdling milk, to kidnapping victims and casting evil spells. Fairies are thought to make 'fairy gold', which may entice humans, but which later turns to gingerbread or gorse blossom. Another of their skills is in making 'fairy ointment', which when rubbed on to the eyes, will give a person a supernatural ability to see, though afterwards they may become blind.

The Fairy 'Changelings'

There is a great deal of folklore and superstition about fairies and human children. In many tales, fairies substitute fairy children (changelings) for human ones. The idea of the changeling was often used in medieval times to explain the behaviour or appearance of a difficult, sickly, or ugly child. In particular, mentally retarded or badly behaved children would be thought of as 'changelings'. In another variant of this lore, fairies sometimes substitute an elderly fairy for a human child, so that the fairy will be cosseted and looked after for the remainder of his or her days. Moreover, fairies may exchange their children for human ones to prevent inbreeding, and giving new blood to both races. In a strange parallel to the vampire legend, fairy children need human milk to thrive, and will seek a series of human mothers for sustenance.

In Celtic mythology, fairies are said to live in woodlands, hills, and lonely rural spots where they will not be disturbed by passing humans. They may also live underground, or in rocky places. In some myths, they are thought to be the spirits of rivers or trees, and guards of these enchanted areas, capturing any unfortunate human beings who venture into them, and holding them to ransom. According to legend, there are several kinds of fairies, including 'trooping' fairies, who live in groups, and 'solitary' fairies, who live alone.

Demoted Angels

There are many ancient fairy myths and theories on their origin. Some believe them to be a very old race, predating human life on earth. The idea that they live in an Otherworld in the Western Isles is connected to the story of Avalon in Arthurian legend. In this version, their domain is guarded by a fairy queen with a silver bough who grants safe passage to the human beings travelling by. In Celtic lore, the fairy folk, known as the 'sidhe', live in ancient cairns in country places. They may be worshipped as pagan deities. For example the Irish myth of Tuath De Danann tells of defeated gods and goddesses living in fairy mounds in the hills, who settled there centuries ago. In medieval alchemy, in the works of Paracelsus, fairies are described as 'demoted angels' caught between heaven and hell. They exist in a limbo: not quite good enough for heaven, yet not quite evil enough for hell.

The Fairy Raid: Carrying off a Changeling - Midsummer Eve,
by Sir Joseph Noel Paton, 1867.

ANGELS IN THEOSOPHY

In the theosophy movement, which began in the late 19th century, angels play a very important part. The movement was founded in New York by Helena Petrovna Blavatsky, Henry Steel Olcott, and William Quan Judge. Their theory was that all religions contain a part of the truth, and that through these religions, humanity moves towards enlightenment.

Theosophists also believe that nature is based upon a spiritual or divine nature, and that philosophy, science, art, commerce and philanthropy help us to attain what they call 'the Absolute'. In their view, the universe is made up of spiritual units of consciousness, or Monads, each fulfilling its destiny. These manifest themselves as angels, among other forms.

White Garments of Light

The theosophy movement took ideas from many religions, including Christianity and Buddhism, to create an esoteric picture of the angel. In theosophy, angels are invisible, created as spirit without bodies, with white garments of light, and haloes. They may take bodily form to carry out the work of their consciousness, and when they do, they appear as beautiful, young, androgynous human beings. From readings of the New Testament, the theosophists believed that the faithful may become angelic on Judgement Day; but they cautioned against the idea that angels are dead souls. Instead, they adopted the Eastern idea of a 'recording angel' tallying up the 'karma' possessed by a person at the point of death, and assigning that person a particular realm or sphere of existence, perhaps as an angel, perhaps not, in the afterlife as a result of their good or bad deeds on earth.

Elements of Judaism also make an appearance in theosophy. Blavatsky believed that Christian angelology derived from that of the Pharisees, and came from Babylonia. Biblical angels were seen as 'sons of God' or messengers, some of them fallen angels such as the Nephilim. On the other hand, certain angels were personifications of 'elementals', beings that had come down to earth from ether, and inhabited the bodies of those who called upon them. The theosophists conceived of the material world as being made by inferior angels, the Elohim, who were practical beings. They also believed that mankind was formed from an angelic host which inhabited the people of a certain race and period on earth.

In particular, the archangel Michael was seen as the being who could transform the spiritual realm into the objective realm. Blavatsky described him as leader of the sacred militia, guardian of the planets, king of the stars, and the 'Satan slayer'. She traced his lineage back to the Roman god Mercury.

Planetary and Solar angels

According to Blavatsky, there are two main types of angel or 'deva'. The first kind live in the atmospheres of the planets of the solar system and are called 'Planetary Angels'. The second live inside the sun, and these are known as 'Solar Angels'. Each planetary system has its own set of angels. The angels of each system help to guide basic evolution in their cosmos, and are responsible for governing the process of nature, for example, overseeing the growth of plants, and the balance of the seasons.

Angels, or 'devas', are usually invisible, but they can sometimes be seen by human beings when the 'third eye' is activated. The 'third eye' is an esoteric concept that appears in many spiritual traditions, both in the East and West, and re-fers to a faculty whereby individuals are able to perceive higher spiritual planes that are obscure to most people. These devas witnessed by the third eye are reported to be like coloured flames, but are otherwise similar to human beings, in stature and form. Indeed, the devas may actually be incarnated as human beings, but will be visible to those who have the ability to see through the 'third eye'.

The Elementals

According to theosophy, as well as seeing devas, or angels, people with the 'third eye' faculty are able to see nature spirits, 'elementals' (beings made of ether which have taken bodily form), and fairies. The 'elementals' are beings which have taken a separate line of evolution from human beings: they are made of a rare, fine substance called 'etheric matter', and become such creatures as gnomes, undines (water sprites), sylphs and salamanders. These beings will then reincarnate eventually, and become devas, or angels. The idea of 'elementals' in theosophy is drawn largely from medieval alchemy, described by such writers as Paracelsus.

Helena Petrovna Blavatsky, photographed in 1875.

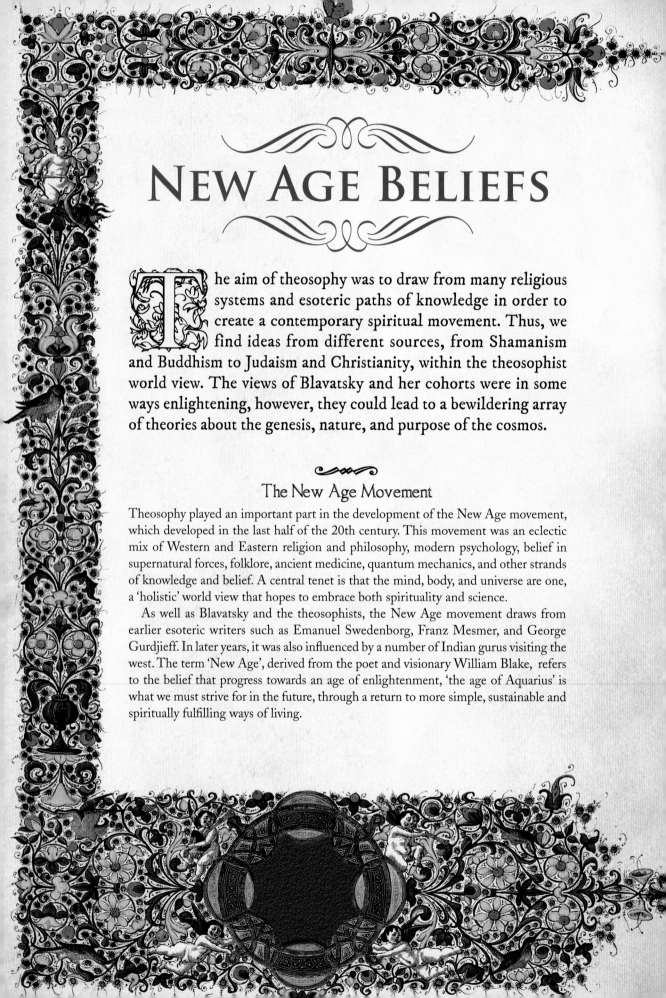

NEW AGE BELIEFS

The aim of theosophy was to draw from many religious systems and esoteric paths of knowledge in order to create a contemporary spiritual movement. Thus, we find ideas from different sources, from Shamanism and Buddhism to Judaism and Christianity, within the theosophist world view. The views of Blavatsky and her cohorts were in some ways enlightening, however, they could lead to a bewildering array of theories about the genesis, nature, and purpose of the cosmos.

The New Age Movement

Theosophy played an important part in the development of the New Age movement, which developed in the last half of the 20th century. This movement was an eclectic mix of Western and Eastern religion and philosophy, modern psychology, belief in supernatural forces, folklore, ancient medicine, quantum mechanics, and other strands of knowledge and belief. A central tenet is that the mind, body, and universe are one, a 'holistic' world view that hopes to embrace both spirituality and science.

As well as Blavatsky and the theosophists, the New Age movement draws from earlier esoteric writers such as Emanuel Swedenborg, Franz Mesmer, and George Gurdjieff. In later years, it was also influenced by a number of Indian gurus visiting the west. The term 'New Age', derived from the poet and visionary William Blake, refers to the belief that progress towards an age of enlightenment, 'the age of Aquarius' is what we must strive for in the future, through a return to more simple, sustainable and spiritually fulfilling ways of living.

Angels of the New Age

There is no fixed set of New Age beliefs, but the concept of a central deity is popular, as is belief in angels or 'devas' as good-natured spiritual forces, sometimes appearing to human beings, or actually being incarnated as human or animal beings. A host of New Age workshops assist in 'identifying early angel experiences' or 'releasing the inner angel'. More specifically, certain spiritual leaders promise to put individuals in touch with particular angels, such as the archangel Michael.

Because of the range of beliefs and ideas within the New Age Movement, it is difficult to pin down exactly what a New Age angel is. In most cases, the angel will be kind, non-judgemental, and helpful. The idea of a comforting presence, such as a guardian angel, continues to be very strong, just as it was in ancient times. People may seek help from angels when they are at an important crossroads in their lives, and need spiritual advice as to which path to take. In addition, the concept of the angel easing the journey to death, and perhaps being present at a person's death bed, remains a powerful one. There is also a strong notion within New Age ideology that the modern individual has begun to reject the intense materialism of world capitalism, and craves spiritual nourishment, which can perhaps be better provided by a belief in angels rather than a fully-fledged commitment to religious traditions that are seen as outmoded, oppressive, and reactionary.

Ascended Masters

New Age practitioners may believe in the existence of 'Ascended Masters', who have a similar function to angels as spiritual guides. The concept of the 'Ascended Master' comes from theosophy, where the idea was propounded that some very enlightened human beings undergo a process of spiritual transformation. An 'Ascended Master' becomes a godlike being and a source of unconditional divine love, uniting with the great 'God Self'. Once these Masters become spirit, they attend to the needs of humanity, inspiring and motivating spiritual growth. 'Ascended Masters' include such famous religious teachers as Jesus, Buddha, and Confucius, but there are also many teachers who become spirits like angels, descending to offer humanity their guidance when occasion demands.

Goal Attainment

In common with general New Age ideas about positive thinking, some practitioners suggest that in order to gain what we want in life, we must openly declare our desires to the angels. When we do this, we must try to think in a considerate, rather than selfish way, taking into account the welfare of others as well as ourselves. Thus, for example, if we want to become rich and successful, we must show how this will benefit those around us, and take care not to wish for material goods simply to indulge ourselves. If the angels deem our plans worthy, they will gather to discuss them, and may decide to help us achieve them if they see fit.

Brain Programming

One of the more unusual beliefs of some New Age practitioners is that angels can help human beings by becoming 'brain programme editors'. This involves the angels becoming tiny light waves in order to access the neurotransmitters in our brain cells. When the angels, as small particles of light, go into our brains, they flood them with energy, helping us to transform negative thoughts into positive ones. Brain cells that are addicted to negative thinking can be re-routed to engage in free, positive ways of conceiving the world and our place in it. This will have beneficial effects on the way we think and engage with others in our daily lives.

The Storm Spirits, by Evelyn De Morgan, 1900.

COMMUNING
WITH ANGELS

Making Contact with Angels

Angels can be called upon to give us advice or guidance, to bring a sense of peace into our lives, or the lives of people we love. Learning how to contact them whenever we need them can be a delightful process and forms an important part of our relationship with our heavenly helper.

Contacting Your Angel

There are many ways of making contact with angels. These methods include channelling, prayer, meditation, writing letters, using crystals, or through colour therapy. Before you start, it is important to create the correct environment in which to commune with angels. A room free of clutter, with open windows and positive energy will encourage the angels to receive your messages.

Channelling the Angel

Channelling, or spiritism, is a form of making contact in which the 'channeller' offers 'angel listenings' to his or her clients. The client visits the channeller, or perhaps communicates by telephone or the internet, in an encounter that lasts 20 to 30 minutes. During this time, the channeller will enter into a trance and write down everything the angel is saying, using a pen and paper. The channeller will then relay this information to the client. The client will not see the angel, but reports claim that a presence, or glow of light, has been seen while this process is taking place. Channellers, many of whom advertise on the internet, often stress that angels offer 'unconditional love', are non-judgemental, and bring great joy, light and love, into the lives of the people who encounter them. Some channellers offer contact with specific angels, for example the Archangels Metatron, Azrael, and Chamuel (all Judaic angels), and help with particular problems or areas ruled by these angels. Some channellers may hold strong Christian or other traditional religious beliefs, but many do not, preferring to take a more open spiritual approach.

Creating an Angel Altar

The age-old idea of praying to the angel continues to be popular in the 21st century. Building an angel altar will create the perfect space to pray to an angel. Pick an area that is generally quiet and transform a shelf or small table into a dedicated area for angelic communication. Cover the shelf or small table with fabric in your favourite colour. As you will find out, colours

Your angel may bring you joy, light and love.

have a special significance with particular angels, so the colour of the fabric may affect which angel you attract. Clear the surrounding area of clutter and rubbish, ensuring the energy in the room cannot be tainted by distracting influences. Adorn the altar with personal objects that are special or beautiful, such as angelic figurines, stones, crystals, and items you have received from the angels such as pennies and feathers. Burning incense or essential oils such as sandalwood, rose and jasmine may help entice the angels to you. If you have a private garden, a peaceful corner is an excellent location for an angel altar. Being close to nature and out in the fresh air will help you clear your head, and may help you concentrate better. Spend a few minutes each day at the altar and bring only positive energy to it. Close your eyes and speak to the angels, either aloud or in your head. They may answer through sending you a sign from above, in your sleep or perhaps in the form of a physical encounter. Speak to the angels often; the more frequently you commune with them, the stronger your relationship will become.

Meditation and Visualization

Connected to the process of prayer is that of meditation or visualization, in which a person may, through clearing the mind to produce an altered state of consciousness, be able to make contact with an angel. Before you start, it is important that your mind and body is clear of the effects of drugs, alcohol, caffeine and even sugar. Morning is recommended as the best time to meditate. Withdraw to a quiet room and position yourself in a comfortable way. Perhaps you have a favourite chair that holds some special significance, or you may choose to lie down on your bed, or on the floor with a pillow under your head. Relax, close your eyes, and take deep breaths rhythmically, counting may help you do this. Imagine a ring of white light around your body, protecting you and pushing any bad feelings away. Try and breathe this ring into you, so you are absorbing the white light. Now take your attention away from the physical world and open your perception to the spiritual world. When this happens, you should be able to make contact with an angel. The process of visualization will help – this is simply picturing the angel you wish to commune with; having an image in mind will keep your focus and encourage an angel to receive you. If you struggle to visualize your angel, try imagining a brilliant ray of light, or beautiful angel wings around you. Although you can do this anywhere that feels comfortable to you, try meditating at your angel altar the first time, as you will have a special connection there.

Letter Writing

Another way of communing with the angelic realm is via letter writing. It can be helpful to create a peaceful environment to do this in. Play some music that relaxes you, light some candles or burn some incense or essential oils. Use a new piece of paper and a favourite pen or pencil, date the letter and address it, 'Dear Angel'. Some people find it helpful to cut the paper into an angelic shape, such as wings, to help them get into the angelic zone. Write freely, without fear of being judged or censured. The tone should be friendly; imagining you are writing to your best friend should help get you in the right frame of mind. Write down your anxieties, through this process you will start to feel more relaxed. By putting your issues down on a piece of paper, you are outlining your problems in a clear and concise way, and will then be ready to pass these burdens over to your angelic friends. 'Post' your letter where you feel it won't be disturbed or tampered with, ideally it should be placed on your angel altar for them to read. You could also leave the letter under your pillow, in the same way a tooth would be left for the tooth fairy. Alternatively, you can burn the letter outside, using a white candle. This way, the angels receive the letter in the form of ashes. Obviously, you must be very careful if you decide to do this. Remember to thank the angels once they have given you the reply you were seeking, you can do this in the form of another letter.

If you struggle with writing a letter, another option is to make an angel card. This is much like a greeting card, but it doesn't need to have any words on it. Treat it like a collage and get creative. It can have whatever you like on it; bows, sequins, photos, pieces of material such as lace, ribbons, buttons; or cut-outs of words that inspire you perhaps. There are no limits and no rules, simply allow yourself to be drawn to certain colours or fabrics and glue it all together to create a focus point on your angel altar.

Crystal Therapy

Crystals are a useful tool to call down angels and also have the added bonus of healing properties. Each type of crystal has a unique internal structure that gives out a resonance at a certain frequency. This 'vibrational resonance', as it is called, is said to help restore the body's balance, and is used to heal anything from minor ailments to serious illnesses, by working holistically to harmonize the mind, body and spirit, restoring stability to the body's natural healing mechanisms. Crystals are worn as pendants, or may be swept over the body as crystal wands or pendulums. They may also be carved into the shape of angels or other spiritual beings. Many websites advertise 'pocket angels', small angels carved from such crystals as amethyst, emerald, jade, rose quartz, and turquoise, which are believed to have special healing properties.

The crystals and stones used in angel therapy each have different powers. The crystals are separated into colours, and individual powers belong to each group.

RED = ruby, garnet, red jasper and bloodstone boost energy levels.

ORANGE = citrine, topaz, carnelian and amber increase creativity and sensuality.

YELLOW = tiger's eye, citrine and ametrine encourage confidence and release tension.

GREEN AND PINK = emerald, jade, rose quartz and kunzite promote compassion and unconditional love.

BLUE = blue lace agate, turquoise and aquamarine inspire expression and communication.

INDIGO = lapiz lazuli, tanzamnite and iolite open up our intuition.

VIOLET = selenite, charoite and amethyst allow us to connect with our higher selves.

BLACK AND BROWN = smoky quartz, obsidian and black tourmaline provide protection and grounding.

Choosing Your Crystal

When choosing a crystal, pick the one which first draws your attention. When you hold your chosen crystal it may feel unusually warm or cold, and may also feel as though it is pulsing with its own energy, making your hands tingle. These sensations are not experienced by all, so do not worry if the crystal does not trigger any odd feelings.

If you do not immediately become drawn to a crystal, do not fret – sometimes the crystal picks us. Give it a few minutes and think hard about what you want to gain from the experience the crystal gives you, then the crystal you are destined to have should speak to you.

Some crystals are described as being blessed or activated through meditation with a particular angel, who can be communicated with by holding the crystal in the palm of your hand and asking for the vibration to flow from the angel. The stone then becomes permanently charged and can attract the angel any time thereafter. Keep your crystal collection on your angel altar, where it can continue to enhance the angel energy around this sacred space.

Essential Oils

An angel altar is not complete without some angelic essential oils burning. These delicate fragrances have the ability to heighten our consciousness and make it easier for us to receive the presence or influence of the angels. Essential oils are pure, there is nothing nasty added to them, and this adds to their angelic appeal. Because of their purity, they possess the ideal energy for spiritual use.

There are several ways to use essential oils. You could put a drop on your palms and rub them together, and then sit in the prayer position. Using candles is an effective method too. Light a candle and wait for a small amount of wax to melt, then blow it out. Add three drops of essential oil to the melted wax and re-light the candle. If you do this, be careful not to spill any oil on the wick as these oils are highly flammable. Another way of releasing the scent is by adding a few drops to a bowl of boiling water. The aroma will be dispersed by the steam and soon the room will be filled. A traditional diffuser is a good method, too. Add a few teaspoons of water and a few drops of essential oil to the bowl at the top of the diffuser. Light the candle and wait for the gentle fragrance to permeate the room.

As each oil has its own power, mixing a couple of oils together can create something very special and personal. When blending your own scent, your mind must be free of any negativity, as this can be passed on to the fragrance. Simply mix a few drops of your chosen oils together in a bowl and transfer to a bottle for use. If you plan to keep the mixture for a long time, store it in an amber-coloured bottle. This will keep the spiritual charge intact. Note that after three months the blend will start to lose its potency and diminish in power.

There are many different oils that blend well together. Sandalwood, for example, is a scent which has a true affinity with the angels, and mixes well with jasmine, a fragrance which encourages optimism and confidence. Marjoram is an excellent oil for those that live in a highly anxious state, and is paired well with cedar-wood, which assists us in diminishing emotional blockages. To create a scent which endeavours to heal emotional wounds, mix rose, which alleviates sorrow and resentment, and blend with ylang ylang, an ingredient which opens up the heart and encourages forgiveness. There are many variations to try, with each essential oil bringing a different quality to your angel altar.

Colour

Certain colours are connected to certain angels, and wearing a particular colour of clothing will attract a particualr angel to you. Adorning your angel altar with fabric in a specific colour has the same effect, so when you come to put your altar together bear this in mind. The colour theme can extend to the ornaments that are placed on your angel altar, such as candles or items of personal significance. The archangels each have special links to colours and are angels of certain qualities.

ARCHANGEL MICHAEL = blue and gold, angel of protection and courage.
ARCHANGEL RAPHAEL = green and pink, angel of healing and unity.
ARCHANGEL CHAMUEL = pink and orange,

angel of unconditional love and compassion.
ARCHANGEL GABRIEL = indigo and white, angel of guidance and inspiration.
ARCHANGEL IOPHIEL = yellow, angel of wisdom and joy.
ARCHANGEL URIEL = gold and purple, angel of peace and devotion.
ARCHANGEL ZADKIEL = violet, angel of mercy and tolerance.

It is worth choosing colours that seem to speak to you. With almost every aspect of communing with angels it is your intuition that you should learn to rely on. Listen to your inner voice and be guided by your instincts.

Angel Cards

Angel, or oracle, cards are sets of illustrated cards that are used, like tarot cards, to make psychic readings, foretell the future and simply ask questions about your life. The cards reveal answers and help us solve our problems. They can be purchased or made at home. Arguably, homemade cards are more effective as they are charged only with your energy. To create your own deck, you need coloured card and pens or pencils. Accessories such as sequins, stars and glitter will make them look more attractive, and may also help capture the angels' attention. There are no rules on how many cards there should be in your deck, some angel experts use as many as 40, and some use a lot less. Generally, angel cards display the name of an angelic quality on each card, or a motivational and inspirational phrase. Brainstorm some words that you associate with angels, for example: courage, faith, harmony, patience, strength or trust. Write each word on a card and illustrate it accordingly. You do not have to be an accomplished artist for this, in fact, a splash of colour that you feel corresponds to the word will suffice! Phrases such as, 'go for it', or 'steady progress', are also appropriate, as we often need a little push towards taking a leap in life. Use keywords such as 'friendship' and 'forgiveness' too, and words that relate to your goals, hopes and dreams.

When your cards are ready, you can begin. Get comfortable and allow yourself to really relax. Breathe in peace and love and dispel any negativity from your mind. Lay all the cards face down in front of you. At this point, you may like to have a question in mind, or be open to some gentle guidance. Close your eyes and take a few minutes to feel yourself connect with the angelic realm. Invite an angel into your life, and when you feel its presence, ask a question or relay any concerns to the angel. Then pick a card – remember, always stick with the card you were first drawn to. Turn the card over and reflect on how the words relate to your problem or situation. If the hidden meaning is not clear right away, take a few moments and the message will eventually reveal itself.

Angelic Affirmations

Another way of getting answers through angel cards is shuffling the deck, asking a question while you do this, and stopping when it feels right. The card you stop on will bring you a message. Once you have picked your card and interpreted the words, keep it with you or display it somewhere so you'll see it often throughout the day and the message will keep being reinforced. If you don't need any specific help or guidance, simply asking the angels, 'how shall I approach today?', is a great way to start the day, as the angel card will charge you with positivity. These cards can also be used as a handy tool to keep you feeling good throughout the day. Keeping one in your pocket, or perhaps copying the words onto post-it notes and leaving them on mirrors around the house, will ensure that the message sinks in. The repetition of affirmations can help deepen your bond with the angels, as you tune more and more into their wavelength.

ANGELOLOGISTS

Angel therapy is offered to those wishing to seek help from above. Through communication with either an individual's guardian angel or one of the archangels, those in need can receive the help they are looking for. The angel therapist does not, in most cases, belong to any recognized religious order, but believes that each person on the planet has a guardian angel, and that these angels perform an assisting role, helping to bring peace, joy, and love into our lives.

DOREEN VIRTUE

One of the major practitioners of angel therapy is Doreen Virtue, who has produced angel cards, written numerous books and offers training courses in angel therapy. Virtue is, according to her website, 'a spiritual doctor of psychology and a fourth-generation metaphysician working with the angelic, elemental and ascended-master realms'. As a child, she was noted for her clairvoyant abilities, but having been teased by friends, she decided to keep quiet about this aspect of her life. However, in 1995, she received a warning from an angel that her car was about to be stolen. She ignored this warning, and went on to park her car. She was then accosted by two men brandishing weapons, who were about to attack her. Her angel instructed her to scream loudly, which she did. Passers-by came to her rescue, thus saving her life. After this, Virtue decided to give her life to receiving and understanding the messages from her angel, who spoke to her in a loud, male voice. She rediscovered the clairvoyant potential that she had experienced earlier in her childhood, and began to look at her training in conventional Western psychology in a new light.

Virtue went on to combine her training in psychology with her experience as a visionary, coming up with the idea of 'angel therapy', in which the power of angels is used to improve people's daily lives. She has recently been quoted as saying: 'When you work with angels, you can lean upon their light to help you heal at miraculous rates and in amazing ways. The angels can help us heal physically, spiritually, emotionally, and financially.'

A Gift from our Creator

As well as seeing clients, running workshops, and writing books, Virtue conducts call-in online radio shows, and has appeared on national television, including Oprah, CNN, Good Morning America, The View with Barbara Walters, Donny & Marie, and Roseanne. She also writes for magazines and newspapers, and features on her work have appeared in the *Los Angeles Times*, *New York Daily News*, and *The Boston Globe*. She claims: 'The angels are with us as a gift from our Creator, and their aim is to establish peace on Earth, one person at a time. Working wing-in-hand with the angels, I believe that this goal is possible. May your inner light burn brightly today, and all the days to come.'

Other authors and teachers of this type include such practitioners as Jacky Newcomb, Diana Cooper, Sanaya Roman, and Steven Farmer. Jacky Newcomb is a British writer who specializes in books about angels, especially angelic contact experiences, afterlife communication with angels, and other experiences of the supernatural. She has published many books and CDs, and has made a documentary about her experiences. She also runs workshops and meditation courses, and appears regularly on television and radio.

Doreen Virtue, angel therapist.

The Angel Craze

Today, there are many angelologists of various kinds – healers, channellers, visualizers, programmers, card readers, crystal gazers, colour therapists, workshop leaders, and so on – offering their wares in magazines, books and on the internet. Interest in angels has soared. No longer are angels simply pictured on Christmas cards, they are the subject of in-depth magazine features and are discussed on radio and TV. A great deal of angel merchandise is available, whether in stores or online: crystals, jewellery, T shirts, calendars, mugs, coins, wishing boxes, bookmarks, worry stones, figurines, statuettes, charms, trinket dishes, 'pocket angels', and so on. Angels are big business, and a great deal of money is made out of them.

In many ways, this is not surprising. We live in a highly commercial culture, and the image of the angel continues to be an attractive, significant one today, as it has been for centuries. It is only natural that individuals the world over, whether children or adults, whether religious believers or not, should take pleasure in objects that remind us of this ancient symbol of hope, love, comfort and joy. However, it does seem that this commercialized 'angel craze', as it has been called, may sometimes obscure the true meaning and history of this important symbol, which crosses many cultures and periods of history, and has a profound message to offer humanity: that of honouring the spiritual aspect of our nature, and trying to keep in touch with it in our daily lives. We may do this, as ancient civilizations did, by building personal shrines or keeping a small image close at hand, for example as a pendant or 'pocket angel', but this should not be seen as a substitute for thought, reflection and study of the real nature of this symbol of the divine, which has endured through time and remains with us in the 21st century.

LEFT: Angel oracle cards, angel statuette, crystals and stones.
RIGHT: A 'pocket angel' card.

SIGNS FROM ABOVE

Angels, being first and foremost messengers, find numerous ways to communicate with us, and using signs or symbols is a classic method. Odd moments, bizarre coincidences and unusual feelings are often the work of the angels. They will try and get our attention any way they can, even going to the effort of shaping clouds, dropping feathers at our feet and playing our favourite song on the radio when we need it.

If we ask the angels a question, they will respond by sending us a celestial sign. It really is as simple as that. Anytime we concentrate on wanting something, really willing and wishing, this is us praying for it. Keeping our desires in mind at all times is part of the process, the harder we wish for something, the more likely the angels will hear us. There are key steps in ensuring the angels will listen to your wishes and deliver you signs. You must ask for a sign, you must have faith and trust in the angels and their powers, and you must be open to receiving their guidance in whatever shape or form they send it in. You may find writing down your desires easier (see page 122), or meditating and visualizing (see page 122) your prayer being answered. Remember that angels do not just exist to give us subtle nods here and there, they are also figures of comfort and peace. They will lift our spirits when we are low, and give us a feeling of companionship when we feel alone or unloved. You can ask the angels for emotional support as well as guidance, and they will make their presence known in a variety of ways.

Clouds

Angels will often send you messages through imagery, and the sky serves as their own blank piece of paper. Clouds sometimes form in particular shapes, for example, in the shape of a pet, or perhaps a face. To the believer, these are obvious and significant – but to cynics, the clouds are merely formless white fluff. It is no coincidence that you may see shapes in the sky that resemble something eventful that has happened in your life. A deceased pet, for example, may appear in the sky in the form of a cloud, this is an angel letting you know he is at peace. Clouds in the shape of angels and hearts are sometimes reported, these are heavenly reminders that you are being watched over.

Dreams

Sometimes we have dreams that are complete nonsense from start to finish, and sometimes we have dreams that covey a real message or perhaps answer questions we've been mulling over for days. The angels can influence your dreams, and can send symbols to you while you sleep, see page 134. Of course, angels can appear as themselves in dreams too, so if you're lucky enough to be visited by an angel in your dream, you must cherish the experience forever.

Feathers

There are few symbols more heavenly than a feather. Of all the signs that angels send to us mere mortals, this is perhaps the most frequently reported. Feathers are intrinsically linked to flight, and their pure, white appearance reminds us of the serene beauty of angel wings. When a feather falls at your feet, it is an angel dropping one down from the sky to remind you that you are not alone. Although a long white feather may look the most angelic, they can appear in different sizes and colours, so do not dismiss a short grey feather! Often, feathers appear at times when you need comfort and support from the angels. If you ask for a sign they will always deliver, and with no bird in the sky to account for the fallen feather, you can be sure it was sent by an angel.

Fragrance

An angel may let you know it is near by suddenly releasing a fragrance. It will most likely be an aroma you have not smelt before, and one that you find hard to describe to others. It will be faint at first, and grow stronger as the angel's proximity to you increases, then the fragrance will disappear as quickly as it arrived. Often, this fragrance will return in times of sadness or despair, and the smell will transport you back to the first time you noticed it, filling you with hope and positivity. Sometimes, and usually when you are feeling low, you will suddenly detect a certain smell that you connect with a deceased loved one, this is a pleasant reminder that this person is always with you, bringing you comfort from beyond.

Intuition

We make numerous decisions everyday, big and small. You may drive home from work one way, and the next day feel that it would be wise to avoid that particular route. There may not be an obvious reason for this change, but you may feel a strong urge inside that you cannot ignore. This is an angel guiding you. You must pay attention to this inner voice or feeling, as an angel may be talking to you to prevent something bad happening. Remember that angels cannot interfere with your free will, so you must also have faith in your own intuition, making decisions in the knowledge that someone is watching over you.

Light

Angels will use many methods to get your attention, and manipulating light is a favourite. They might make electric lights flicker or dim, or send flashes of light across a room or up a wall. If you are struggling internally with something, they may bathe you in natural light for a few seconds. This trickery with light could be quite startling, but remember it is just a friendly reminder that they are nearby.

Music

Angels can communicate with us through sounds, as well as visually. For example, an overplayed song on the radio which gets stuck in your head could actually be an angel wanting you to understand the message in the lyrics. Alternatively, if you already have a song in your head, and then you hear it on the radio or perhaps being sung by a friend, this is confirmation an angel is trying to tell you something. Angels are not naughty by nature, but they do have a slightly mischievous habit of randomly switching objects on. Precious musical boxes, for example, may start to play without being wound up, or a radio might suddenly come alive while a particular song is playing. This may give you a fright at first, but remember to look for the hidden meaning. Pay particular attention to songs with 'angel' in the title or lyrics; these songs are still signs, just a little more obvious than others.

Numbers

Have you ever looked at a digital clock one day, and then the next day, glanced at it at precisely the same time? Then perhaps repeated this the next day, and then the next? Looking at the clock at the same time every day is not coincidence, an angel has been prompting you to do so. The number sequence in the display is significant to you. If it reads 11:11 for example, it could be referring to 11 November, perhaps this is a loved one's birthday, or the anniversary of an event in your past. The numbers added together, i.e 1+1+1+1 = 4, could also give you a message.

Perhaps the number 4 is significant in some way. The angels give us signs, but it is up to us to interpret them. The next time you see recurring number sequences in telephone numbers, license plates or even shopping bills, try and decipher the message behind the code.

Pennies

Money may seem like an odd calling card for an angel, compared to clouds, feathers and dreams, but coins and cash are classic signs from above, and turn up just when they are needed the most. Think of how many times you have been short a few pence at a till and desperately dug into empty pockets, to then discover a shiny 10p piece. The next time you ask the angels for a sign and receive a coin, consider the time and place you found it. Also check the year stamped on it as it will most likely hold some special significance for you, perhaps an anniversary of an event that is close to your heart. This can be the angels' way of telling you that a special date will never be forgotten.

People

Sometimes you may enter into a bad or helpless situation unintentionally. You may be lost, or perhaps your car has broken down in the middle of nowhere. Suddenly, a complete stranger appears and offers you help and comfort, and expects nothing in return. These random acts of kindness are not so random after all: these strangers are actually angels that have been sent to you in your hour of need. If you are blessed with an experience like this, you must remember to thank the angels afterwards and repay them by doing the odd good deed when you can.

Rainbows

Rainbows have a wonderful effect on us, we cannot help but smile when the rain clears and a beautiful band of colour is stretched across the sky.

Rainbows have religious connotations, and are used often to symbolize all things heavenly: love, peace, friendship and support. When a rainbow is sent to you, it conveys that your entire situation is being taken care of by the angels, and that you should let go and allow the angels to sort things out for you. To see several rainbows on one day, or two at the same time is an extra special sign, and a moment that you should treasure.

Sensations

Throughout the day you may experience odd sensations such as feeling someone is in a room with you when you are alone. You may suddenly get a shiver up your spine, butterflies in your stomach or be covered in goosebumps. These are odd sensations which occur so frequently that you do not consider there could be an unusual reason behind them. Angels may affect you gently in these ways, using their presence to influence your thoughts.

Temperature

A sure sign that an angel is in the room with you is if the temperature suddenly alters dramatically. It can become warm, and you can feel the warmth radiating through you. Or it could become cold, and you could feel goosebumps (see above), or a tingling sensation on the back of your neck. A room being hot, and a room being cold, mean the same thing, there is no special message associated with each extreme. The change in the room is enough to let you know that you are in the presence of angels.

Voices

Sometimes angels do not hide the signs in symbols or objects – sometimes they feel like being more direct, and plainly spelling it out for you so there can be no misunderstandings. When you hear these voices and sounds you will understand immediately what their meaning is, and be able to relate it to your problem. Heavenly voices sound different to each person who has experienced them, so try and be open to the different sounds you encounter everyday, and soon you will be able to isolate the voices of angels. Do not be afraid if you hear your name called, turn, and discover that no one is there. That is just your angel letting you know it is near, and that you must not be afraid.

Words

If we directly ask an angel a question, sometimes they can reply in black and white, for everybody to see. Advice, answers, guidance, whatever we are after, can suddenly appear in the form of a headline of a newspaper, and only we will understand the hidden meaning. Books may open on a certain page, begging us to find the passage that speaks to us. In the library, a book may come flying off the shelf and land at our feet, the title being a significant word or phrase.

ANIMAL SYMBOLS IN DREAMS

Symbols can be presented to us at any time of the day, but it may not always occur to us that they are celestial signs and are meant for us to interpret. If we miss these signs, it is likely the angel will try and resend the message when we are asleep. Angels often speak to us in our dreams, either appearing to us in their true form, or using symbols to enlighten or help us.

When we have dreams laden with symbols, they can often seem very poignant, especially if they are particularly vivid or bizarre. It is unknown why the angels choose dreams to speak to us; perhaps it is because when we are asleep we are in a relaxed state, and our minds are open to receive their influence. Some people tend to forget their dreams the second they wake up, and others tend to remember them for days afterwards. Vivid dreams can really stay with us, and we can spend lots of time trying to decipher them. As discussed previously, angels use a variety of symbols, but animal symbols can be the most ambiguous; we often take these at face value, and do not ponder the hidden meaning. Here are some classic animal symbols and their meanings.

Alligator

Generally, the alligator represents danger and scares most people witless. In symbolism, the alligator signifies treachery and deceit. An alligator symbol in a dream tells the dreamer that there is someone in their life causing mischief. Just like the alligator moving undetected through murky waters, the mischief-maker is a crafty manipulator, often gaining trust in order to be accepted, to then be in a better position to strike. A dream featuring an alligator tells the dreamer to be wary and vigilant. If you dream you are trying to escape an alligator, the angels are telling you that there is something that is weighing on your subconscious, and that you must confront it before it is too late.

Bird

Winged creatures, in general, have angelic connotations. With the angels they share feathers and the ability to fly. Birds symbolize freedom as they gracefully traverse the skies, and represent liberation perhaps from a situation, a burden or a secret. They can also symbolize your own goals and aspirations and seeing a bird in your dream can mean that what you desire is in sight, but there is still some work to do. A hawk is believed to signify the presence of a guardian angel and it is considered very lucky to be given this direct sign. If you dream about a hawk, this is your guardian angel telling you it is close by. It also represents your need for comfort and reassurance. A white dove is a symbol of peace, love and innocence, and has special significance in many cultures worldwide. It conjures up ideas of faith and purity, and is used in a variety of organizations as a motif for positivity. White doves appear often in Judaism and Christianity and because of this, they are sometimes used to mark occasions such as weddings, released at the end of the ceremony. White doves have also been released at military funerals in certain parts of the world. While here they are marking a sombre occasion, the white dove persists as a symbol of peace. To dream about two white doves together is symbolic of love and devotion, signifying a good relationship or the beginning of a new one.

Butterfly

One of nature's most beautiful creations, the butterfly is an enduring symbol of freedom, innocence and hope. In some cultures, a pair of butterflies symbolize love, so to see two butterflies at the same time means you are about to enter into a new relationship, or that your current relationship is going well. Butterflies can represent hope, a famous case being the white butterfly seen underground in Chile, as the mines started to cave in (see page 14). How a butterfly could be that far underground and survive the falling rubble as the mines collapsed is a mystery to most, but to believers, the butterfly was an angel in another form, sent to remind the miners not to give up hope. The idiom 'butterflies in the stomach' represents feelings of anxiety or nervousness. The intense fluttering of butterfly wings is comparable to the internal turmoil we suffer when we are really worried or anxious about something. Sometimes, this feeling will come out of nowhere. This is the angels stimulating our intuition, and letting us know that something is not right and that we must follow our instincts. At their simplest, butterflies represent rebirth into a new life as they emerge from their cocoons. Because of this, a butterfly signifies life after death. Seeing a butterfly after a loved one has passed should be interpreted as a message from the deceased, sent to us from above. Famous Swiss psychiatrist Dr Elisabeth Kubler-Ross wrote in her 1991 book *On Life After Death*, 'Death is simply a shedding of the physical body like the butterfly shedding its cocoon.'

Cat

Cats are sometimes associated with bad luck, and those that are superstitious will tend to avoid crossing their path in the street. In fiction, they are often depicted as a witch's familiar, and because of this they have a slightly mysterious edge. In dreams, however, they are sign of intelligence and independence. They also represent intuition, and a cat symbol can be an angel's way of telling you to listen to your inner voice. Cats can, by nature, be aloof and this can tell us to distance ourselves from someone or from a situation. If in the dream they are on the move, this is an angel's way of saying that we should shake up our routine and break some habits, as one of the cats main traits is being resourceful and unpredictable.

Deer

Deer are graceful and beautiful animals. Though big in size, they have a delicate quality which has appealed to generations and led to them being revered in some cultures. In dreams, deer symbolize pride, fertility and peace. In Shamanism, deer are seen as spirit guides, used to lead the souls of the recently deceased to the next world. Because of this, deer are sometimes perceived to be a negative symbol. It can often mean the end of a relationship, and therefore a sign not everyone would be pleased to receive. However, if you see a deer in your dream it may not always be for negative reasons. The concept of the deer as a spirit guide is a common one, and it could mean that your deer is trying to lead you to uncover a hidden talent, or usher you towards taking a new direction in life.

Dolphin

Dolphins have long been connected with angels, and to some, they are seen as angels of the sea. They represent freedom, and if this is restricted in your life, dolphins represent the desire for it. Angels may send us an image of dolphins to remind us that we are free in our decisions and that we should keep the 'bigger picture' in mind. They inspire our sense of adventure and are a positive symbol to see if you are planning on going travelling. Dolphins are believed to be intelligent and sensitive mammals, and they sometimes represent good luck and friendship. A dolphin dream is often an inspirational one, and will be sent to you when you are in need of

guidance in a particular situation, or if you are at a crossroad in life.

Fox

Foxes, in fiction, are often depicted as cunning and sly. In reality, they are seen as a common pest; shady characters that creep around at night infiltrating dustbins and trawling through rubbish for our leftovers. In dreams, foxes symbolize a warning, deception, resourcefulness and intelligence. This could mean a number of things; that you need to be wary of someone, or that you need to become more cunning and shrewd in a situation. A fox can also represent isolation, and your desire for space to reflect on life. An angel may send you this symbol to prompt you to take some time out for yourself and re-evaluate things.

Lion

Lions, traditionally known as the 'King of the Jungle', symbolize strength, courage, authority, beauty and power. The appearance of a lion in your dream can represent many things. There may be an authority figure in your life to whom you do not show enough respect. The angels will send you this sign to remind you to work on these issues with authority and power. You may also get sent a lion symbol to let you know you are being preyed upon, and that you are in a strong position to defend yourself. Finally, a lion is a symbol of something in your life that needs to be tamed. It could be a temper, a hedonistic lifestyle or emotions that feel out of control. The angels will place a lion in your dream to prompt you to take control of the wild aspect of your life.

Monkey

Monkeys are intelligent and sensitive creatures. Because of their lively nature they are perceived as being somewhat mischievous. In dreams, a monkey can represent your silly side and this could be interpreted as an angel telling you that you should try and be more serious. A group of monkeys signal a happy event looming, perhaps a party or a wedding. A group of misbehaving monkeys represent your feelings of anxiety towards the event, such as worrying that something will go wrong. The angels do not tell you the future, that is why you should not take this symbol to heart. It simply means that you should keep a level head and try not to worry.

Owl

Much like the fox, the owl has been represented many times in fiction as a strong character. Owls are often portrayed as being wise and slightly mysterious. In dreams, owls mean wisdom, mystery and transition. Seeing an owl may mean that your life is about to change in some way. If you are debating whether to go into further education, or perhaps retake an exam, an owl is a sign to encourage you to do this. However, if you hear an owl hooting in your dream, this can signal that some disappointment is coming your way, and the angels are trying to prepare you for it.

Unicorn

Unicorns are mythological creatures resembling horses. They are usually white, have a single horn extending from their forehead and often have wings. They are associated with magic and luck, and symbolize wisdom, intelligence, integrity, healing and eternal life. Therefore, a unicorn sign can be a positive one, representing your strength of character. If you are worried about an awkward situation, a unicorn should bring you comfort, and remind you that integrity is more important than pettiness. Angels may also send you this sign to encourage your connection to the spirit realm, and to inspire your interest in this subject.

White Rabbit

A white rabbit can indicate many things: a new baby in the family (particularly if the rabbit is hopping), fertility, rebirth, and good luck. To see multiple rabbits conveys good fortune in your life, and reminds you that you are very lucky. If you see multiple hopping rabbits in your dream, this could mean there are several new additions to the family on the horizon, perhaps twins, or triplets! Rabbits are intrinsically linked to spring and Easter, and if you have strong connections and special memories attached to these, the angels may send you a rabbit sign just to remind you of this time of year.

White Swan

White swans are a classic symbol of love and romance. They mate for life, and when two look at each other their faces together form a perfectly symmetrical heart. It is not, therefore, surprising that they are associated with love, peace and serenity. To see a swan in your dream can symbolize your romantic life. To see a pair, much like with the butterfly and white dove, can mean your love life will see some improvements imminently. An angel may present the swan symbol encouraging us to form bonds with those we admire, and to make the effort to build our relationships into long-lasting friendships.

Wolf

To have a wolf prowling around in a dream can seem like a bad omen, but actually they symbolize pride, confidence, virtue and loyalty. Seeing a wolf can mean an angel is encouraging your feelings of self-worth and reminding you of your high integrity. If you are feeling vulnerable or threatened in a situation, the wolf is a symbol of reassurance and comfort, and you should feel a confidence boost from this. Wolves, in some parts of the world, are revered for their inherent power and close proximity to nature. They are seen as spirit guides, much like the deer, and should be interpreted as a symbol of guidance. If you are about to embark on a physical or spiritual journey, the wolf is an excellent symbol to receive.

ANGELS OF THE IMAGINATION

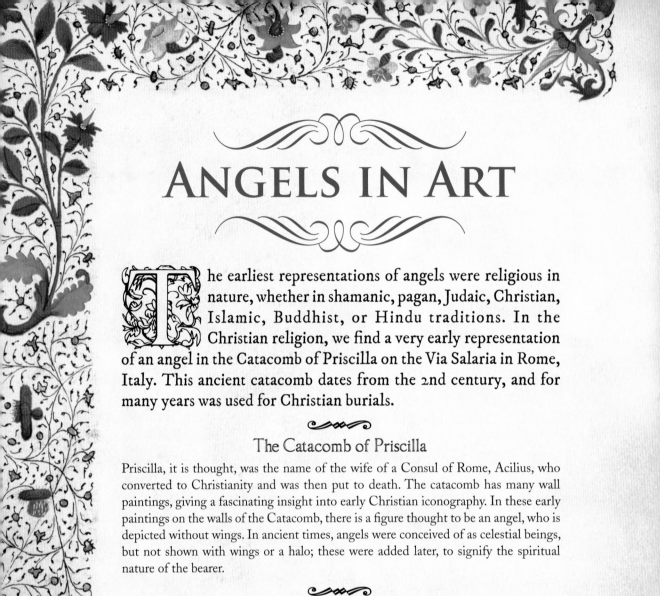

ANGELS IN ART

The earliest representations of angels were religious in nature, whether in shamanic, pagan, Judaic, Christian, Islamic, Buddhist, or Hindu traditions. In the Christian religion, we find a very early representation of an angel in the Catacomb of Priscilla on the Via Salaria in Rome, Italy. This ancient catacomb dates from the 2nd century, and for many years was used for Christian burials.

The Catacomb of Priscilla

Priscilla, it is thought, was the name of the wife of a Consul of Rome, Acilius, who converted to Christianity and was then put to death. The catacomb has many wall paintings, giving a fascinating insight into early Christian iconography. In these early paintings on the walls of the Catacomb, there is a figure thought to be an angel, who is depicted without wings. In ancient times, angels were conceived of as celestial beings, but not shown with wings or a halo; these were added later, to signify the spiritual nature of the bearer.

The Sarcophagus of Junius Bassus

There is also an early representation of an angel on a marble sarcophagus, that of Junius Bassus, an ancient Roman politician, which is now in the Museum of St Peter's Basilica in the Vatican. This heavily carved sarcophagus dates from the year 359, and is one of the oldest burial receptacles of its type, showing intricate scenes on a variety of Christian themes, drawn from both the Old and New Testaments. As Junius Bassus was an important man, he would have had the best sculptors of the period to design and carve his marble coffin, and it is indeed a marvel of the sculptor's art.

One of the scenes from the Bible shown on the sarcophagus is the famous sacrifice of Isaac, in which Abraham received an order from God to kill his son, and was,

naturally enough, tempted not to obey it. In this scene, an angel stands by as Abraham makes his decision, but again, it is depicted without wings. The angel is shown as a youthful, beardless male figure, and looks quite similar to depictions of Christ that also adorn the sarcophagus. However, in other places, the sarcophagus is carved with winged angels, perhaps showing a transition, at this time, from one view of angels as wingless, to another – our familiar modern angel, who always has a large pair of wings to identify him or her as a 'celestial being'.

THE ROMAN ANGEL

Angels in early Christian art, prior to the Romans, were usually shown without wings. It is believed that the wings began to appear as artists and sculptors began to study the Bible, taking account of descriptions within the canonical texts. Influences from the Roman pantheon of gods, in particular winged gods and goddesses such as Hermes and Nike, also contributed to this development.

Early Christian catacomb painting entitled *Woman in Orant Pose*.

On another important sarcophagus, known as the Prince's Sarcophagus, discovered at Sariguzel near Istanbul in the 1930s, we also find representations of angels with wings.

It was not until the end of the 4th century in Christian art that angels began to be regularly depicted as having wings, largely as a result of artists studying religious texts, especially mystical ones, and following the descriptions they found there. For example, in the *Second Book of Enoch*, there is a specific reference to angels as having wings:

And there appeared to me two men, exceeding big, so that I never saw such on earth; their faces were shining like the sun, their eyes too were like a burning light, and from their lips was fire coming forth, with clothing and singing of various kinds. In appearance purple, their wings were brighter than gold, their hands whiter than snow.

The Angels Get Wings

The *Book of Enoch* was not accepted as having much authority in the Christian church, since it was seen as a form of Jewish mysticism that had little to do with the mainstream teaching of the New Testament. However, it seems likely that Christian artists derived many of their ideas from this unorthodox text, and from others like it. By drawing in features from the Roman gods as well, these artists and sculptors came up with the iconic representation of the modern-day winged angel. In addition, the artists' understanding of the angel as a messenger flying between heaven and earth, derived from the Bible, would have suggested the idea of wings, since this would only have been possible if the angels were able to take flight, like birds.

Sculptors and artists were beginning to represent angels with wings in churches and holy places, though the priests and theologians of the period did not actually believe that angels literally had wings. Rather, they taught that the wings were used as a symbol of the divine, so that the angels could be identified, and differentiated from ordinary mortals, as celestial beings. In the same way, the halo, which we also find appearing in Christian iconography, also symbolized the fact that the figure shown was an angel or saint, not simply a mere mortal.

St John Chrysostom

An early Greek Archbishop, St John Chrysostom, who lived between 349 and 407, explained the significance of the angels' wings thus:

'They manifest a nature's sublimity. That is why Gabriel is represented with wings. Not that angels have wings, but that you may know that they leave the heights and the most elevated dwelling to approach human nature. Accordingly, the wings attributed to these powers have no other meaning than to indicate the sublimity of their nature.'

St John Chrysostom was an important early church father, known for his gift of public speaking, and for his stern views on corruption and abuse of church authority. (He was also famous for his anti-Semitic sermons, which were very influential.) After his death, he was given the Greek surname 'chrysostomos', meaning 'golden-mouthed'. His views would have been taken seriously during his lifetime, and would also have been widely known.

Like many church leaders before him, notably Zoroaster, St John Chrysostom believed in angels, but it is clear that he saw them as essentially spiritual and conceptual in nature – as heavenly spiritual messengers from God, not literally winged human-like creatures. However, he also understood, as did Zoroaster and the Jewish patriarchs before him, that Christian artists need to represent the angels in a form ordinary people could understand. This is why angels in the Western tradition, in public places such as churches and other sites of worship, began to be depicted as figures with wings, and why today we think of wings and haloes as essential features of the angel.

BYZANTINE ANGELS

The era of the Byzantine church between 400 AD and 600 AD was a very creative one in the history of angel art. During this time, the Greek and Roman winged gods and goddesses were adapted more and more cleverly into the Christian icon of the angel. In particular, stunning images of the seraphim with its six wings began to appear; wonderful examples can be found in mosaics in the Greek Orthodox Church. There are also some very beautiful mosaics showing angels with wings in the Basilica of St Mary Major in Rome. Later, seraphim sculptures in the 18th-century Anglican church, were adapted from the Byzantine tradition, and this extraordinary six-winged image of the angel found its way into much medieval art.

The Byzantine Archangel Michael

The archangel Michael in military dress was one of the favourite subjects of Byzantine religious artists. The angel was shown wearing a knee-length tunic and an armoured breast plate. Sometimes he was depicted wearing the uniform of the Byzantine emperor's bodyguard, which consisted of an ankle-length tunic and a garment called the 'loros' (a gold vestment encrusted with jewels) that was only worn by the emperor's family and personal guards.

In the middle ages in Europe, from about the 12th century to the 16th, angel imagery continued to follow the basic formula set in Byzantine times. There were, of course, variations according to the artists' individual styles and abilities, but in essence, the main features of the Byzantine angel remained the template for church iconography. Angels were often shown wearing long robes and sometimes the vestments of a man of the church, especially the deacon, wearing a cope (a long mantle or cloak) over a dalmatic (a wide-sleeved tunic).

THE ANNUNCIATION

In the middle ages, angels became a popular subject for religious paintings. The biblical scene in which the angel Gabriel visits the Virgin Mary to announce that God wishes her to be the mother of Jesus was painted many times by different artists. The scene features in the repertoire of almost all the great artists of both the middle ages and the Renaissance. Because of the symmetry of the two figures, the angel and Mary, the scene was often presented as a diptych or, sometimes, as a decorated arch above a doorway. In Eastern Orthodox traditions, the Annunciation often appears on the doorway leading from the nave of the church into the sanctuary, or consecrated area of the church around the altar. As well as painting and sculpture, the Annunciation was depicted in mosaics and stained glass.

Many painters took the Annunciation as their subject, including Sandro Botticelli, Leonardo da Vinci, Michelangelo Caravaggio and Bartolome Murillo. We also find it in the mosaics of Pietro Cavallini in the Santa Maria in Trastevere in Rome, in the frescoes of Giotto di Bondone Padua's Scrovegni Chapel, and in Domenico Ghirlandaio's fresco for the Florentine church of Santa Maria Novella. Also in Florence is Donatello's gilded sculpture at the church of Santa Croce, dated 1435.

One of the most fascinating and mysterious paintings of the Annunciation comes from the hand of the Dutch painter Jan Van Eyck, which is thought to have been painted around the year 1434. The Latin inscription on it reads the greeting of the Angel Gabriel, 'Hail, full of grace' to which Mary replies, 'Behold the handmaiden of the Lord'. Mary's words are painted upside down,

Sense of Sight, Annie Louisa Swynnerton, 1895.

apparently so that God can read them. Mary, in keeping with the medieval view of the mother of God, is depicted as a studious woman who is reading a large book when the angel arrives. She wears a robe in her traditional colour of blue, and in this painting it is given an ermine trim, which suggests that she is of royal blood. Some scholars have also suggested that the features of her face are modelled on those of Isabella of Portugal. Mary's beauty is outshone by that of the angel. The medievals would have tried to make Mary look as chaste as possible, since she is a mortal woman; however, the angel is permitted to be very beautiful, since he is a heavenly being, and as such sexless. The idea was that making Mary very beautiful might have caused inappropriate thoughts in the viewer, which would conflict with her virginal status, whereas the angel was not a being that would be lusted after. Neither of the figures wear a halo, since these were being phased out of Dutch art of the period, because of an emphasis on painting religious subjects in a realistic way. Mary's posture, although modest, is quite ambiguous, and it is hard to tell whether she is kneeling, standing, or sitting.

ANGELS OF THE RENAISSANCE

In the Renaissance period in Italy, much attention was paid to the Classical form, especially in sculpture. The angel was revived, and appeared in many guises, but usually in similar form to the Greek sculptures of antiquity. The icon of the angel continued through the Baroque and Rococo periods in art essentially unchanged, although the depictions of angels and heavenly scenes reached a new complexity.

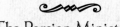

The Persian Miniatures

Meanwhile, outside Europe, winged angels also became an essential part of the religious iconography of Islam. From the 14th century, the myth of the buraq, a magical horse who carried the prophets up to heaven, was depicted in Persian miniatures. The buraq was said to have carried the prophet Muhammad from Mecca to Jerusalem and back during the 'Night Journey' described in the Qur'an. It also carried Muhammed up to heaven, in a similar story to the Christian ascension. The buraq combines elements of other mythical creatures such as the sphinx, the centaur, and the griffin, and we find traces of all of these in the art of the period, where the buraq is sometimes pictured as a winged steed.

The Japanese Winged Spirit

In the Japanese tradition, we find winged human forms that are used to illustrate the characteristics of spirits, both good and evil. In Japanese religion, spirits are treated in a down-to-earth way which is reflected in their stories and their art. The 19th-century artist Yoshitoshi Taiso made a series of paintings called 'Tsuki Hyakushi' ('One Hundred Aspects of the Moon') showing a young woman, Iga-no-Tsubone, meeting a winged spirit named Sasaki Kiyotaka. This spirit was troubled, since he had lost in battle during his lifetime and had been forced to take his own life. The maiden, who is shown as having very long, dark hair, soothes him with her words, and he goes on his way. The scene takes place under moonlight, and the spirit is shown as having large wings.

THE ANGEL OF EMPIRE

By the end of the 19th century in Europe, the angel had become well established as a symbol of state authority. In the Victorian era, there were many ostentatious sculptures featuring angels, and these were used to decorate tombs and memorial statues to members of the royal family, the aristocracy, and important dignitaries. One such example is the Victoria Memorial in London, which stands outside the royal

Music Making Angel with Violin, by Melozzo da Forli, 1480.

residence, Buckingham Palace. Completed in 1911, the memorial has a large statue of Queen Victoria at the centre. Around her, on the other sides of the monument are the angel of justice, the angel of truth, and the angel of charity. On top is the angel of victory, with two seated figures. There are also figures with a nautical theme, such as mermen and mermaids, all alluding to the power and might of the British empire, which Queen Victoria presided over for the best part of a century.

Angels also became a symbol of empire and patriotic fervour in France, with angels adorning the Arc de Triomphe, which is situated at the top of the Champs-Elysées. This colossal monument was designed by Jean Chalgrin in 1806, and inspired by the Roman Arch of Titus, became one of the most famous public monuments in Europe. The trend towards pomp, circumstance, and angels continued well into the 20th century, with grand sculptures such as the gilded Sherman Monument, a tribute to William Tecumseh Sherman, one of

Victoria Memorial, Buckingham Palace, London.

the most renowned generals of the Civil War, by Augustus Saint-Gaudens. The general is shown on horseback, being led by a winged angel. This was one of Saint-Gaudens' most ambitious and technically demanding projects and can be found in Central Park, New York.

Bethesda Fountain

Also in Central Park is the Bethesda Fountain, situated near the infamous lake. The fountain is a key piece in the sprawling 843-acre park, and forms part of the larger Bethesda Terrace attraction, located at the lower of the two terrace levels. In the middle of the fountain is a bronze sculpture of a female winged angel who stands 8ft (2.4m) in height. She is positioned on top of the fountain, where water cascades into an upper basin and spills down into the 'pool'. Beneath her are four 4ft (1.2m) putti, representing temperance, peace, purity and health. The sculpture was designed by Emma Stebbins in 1868, and she was the first female to receive a public commission for a major work of art in the city. The sculpture is also known as *Angels of the Waters*, in reference to the *Gospel of John*, chapter five, which mentions an angel blessing the Pool of Bethesda with healing powers. The sculpture symbolizes the purifying of the city's water supply when the Croton Aqueduct opened in 1842. For this reason the angel holds a lily in one hand, and she blesses the water with the other. The angel and her putti were unveiled to the public in 1873, and the name of the landmark was changed from The Water Terrace to Bethesda Terrace. More than 25 million visitors pass through Central Park each year, and this area is a 'must see' for any tourists.

El Angel de la Independencia

In 1902 a landmark was constructed to commemorate the centennial of the beginning of Mexico's War of Independence, on the order of President Porfirio Diaz. French-Italian sculptor Enrique Alciati took inspiration from the Greek legend of Nike, the winged goddess who symbolizes strength and power. At the top of a 148ft (45m) victory column sits the main feature, a winged angel wearing a robe which is positioned to look as if it is moving in the wind. The angel holds a crown in one hand, and a broken chain in the other, a representation of freedom. She has one foot on the top of the column, and the other slightly raised behind her, as if she is running. The sculpture is made of bronze and in 2006 it was coated in gold. It is situated on a roundabout which looks down boulevard Paseo de la Reforma, a road which stretches out for 7.5 miles (12km). The landmark is commonly known as 'El Angel', and over the years has become a cherished icon to the people of Mexico City.

Angels of the New Millennium

Today, angels are more popular than ever before. They are used a great deal in all forms of Christian and New Age iconography, and also in advertising, to sell anything from lingerie to house cleaning products. Similarly, the word 'angel' is used for businesses providing all kinds of services, often with logos to match. Not surprisingly, many of these depictions of angels are less than artistically satisfying, but it cannot be denied that they reference the great art of the past; and whatever their limitations, they continue to bear witness to the extraordinary hold that the angel has had over the human imagination for centuries. Besides the plethora of angels to be seen in advertising and commercial art, we find an explosion of angel iconography in Christmas products – whether greetings cards, tree decorations, advent calendars, nativity scenes, decorations, or wrapping paper. Stick-on angel wings made of netting and wire, together with dresses, and haloes, have also become popular, not only for children but for adults. These are worn not just at Christmas parties, but at pop festivals and other public events throughout the year.

FAMOUS ANGELS

Our image of the angel today, whether we know it or not, comes from many beautiful paintings and sculptures over a long period of human history.

The Ecstasy of Saint Teresa

This sculpture by Gian Lorenzo Bernini is in the Cornaro Chapel of Santa Maria della Vittoria in Rome. Completed in 1652, it shows a swooning nun being visited by an Angel with a spear. The image comes from an event described by the Carmelite nun Teresa of Avila in her autobiography, where she records her vision of the angel:

I saw in his hand a long spear of gold, and at the iron's point there seemed to be a little fire. He appeared to me to be thrusting it at times into my heart, and to pierce my very entrails; when he drew it out, he seemed to draw them out also, and to leave me all on fire with a great love of God. The pain was so great, that it made me moan; and yet so surpassing was the sweetness of this excessive pain, that I could not wish to be rid of it. The soul is satisfied now with nothing less than God. The pain is not bodily, but spiritual; though the body has its share in it. It is a caressing of love so sweet which now takes place between the soul and God, that I pray God of His goodness to make him experience it who may think that I am lying.

To show that this is a supernatural event, St Teresa is shown lying on a cloud, and above are frescoes of baby angels, or putti, shown flying about in the sky with a white dove, symbolizing the holy ghost. The entire scene is cleverly illuminated by natural light filtering through a hidden window, which is emphasized with gilded rays fashioned in stucco on the walls. Witnesses to the event, including the Cornaro family, are represented by reliefs in what look like theatre boxes around the walls. The central figures of St Teresa and the angel are made of white marble, to reinforce the heavenly nature of the scene, while the figures in the theatre boxes appear in coloured marble. Various commentators, from art historians to philosophers, have commented on the look of intense physical pleasure on the nun's face. Some have seen this as representing

Ecstasy of St. Theresa, by Giovanni Lorenzo Bernini, 1652.

the moment of orgasm, and indeed, St Teresa's description of her meeting the angel seems to have had a very sexual aspect, with the thrusting of the spear, and so on. In our modern-day world, after the teachings of Freud, most people would not be shocked at the idea that the nun's vision of the angel with the spear is an obviously repressed form of sexual longing on the part of a woman without any access to sexual experience.

However, it is not at all clear that Bernini would have held this view, or that he meant to portray the nun in a state of sexual climax. Art historians have been at pains to explain that the way Bernini shows the nun and the angel, in white marble, bathed in heavenly light, and in a completely different, almost surreal space as compared to the onlookers sculpted around the walls, means that he did regard St Teresa as having had an entirely celestial, spiritual experience during her vision, not an earthly, sensual one. However, it is also true that he represented this spiritual experience in earthly terms so that the human spectator could understand it, by giving her a look of pure ecstasy on her face.

❧❧❧

The Sopo Archangels

Another famous work from the 17th century is a set of oil paintings from the Spanish colonial era of Colombia, South America, which today can be seen in the Church of the Divine Saviour in Sopo. The artist is unknown, but they are believed to have been painted around 1650. Some art historians have guessed that they are the work of Colombian painters Bernabe de Posadas or Baltasar de Figueroa, others that the Ecuadorian painter Miguel de Santiago may have been responsible for them. The canvasses show 11 archangels, and one guardian angel. On each of the canvasses is a Hebraic title with the name of the angel depicted, plus some descriptive material in Spanish. In recent years, the Colombian government have developed a programme of restoration for the paintings, which are part of the country's valuable national heritage.

The paintings show the following angels: Ariel, whose name means 'Command of God' and who is the archangel of divine war; Baraquel, Blessing of God, the archangel of virtue; Esriel, Justice of God, the archangel of divine discipline; Gabriel, Strength of God, the archangel of divine salvation; Jehudiel, Penance of God, the archangel of divine hope; Laruel, Mercy of God, the archangel of divine mercy; Michael, the Image of God, the archangel of divine triumph against evil; Raphael, Medicine of God, the archangel of divine healing; Seactiel, the Prayer of God, the archangel of divine serenity; and Uriel, the Fire of God, the archangel of divine wrath. Also pictured are the Guardian angel, who guards little children, and Liadh, the sun of justice, whose function is somewhat obscured because of damage to the painting.

Just as in the Old Testament, the angels are conceived of as different aspects or characteristics of God, coming down to earth to do the divine will, and taking a form that human beings can understand. Each of the figures is life-sized and clothed in rich garments, full of drapes and folds, and featuring large white wings, holding or wearing the symbols of their task. Interestingly, they are mainly shown as almost androgynous: they are ostensibly male figures but they have round hips, and soft, pretty faces. Today, The Sopo Archangels are considered to be one of the great mysteries of Colombian art, and speculation continues regarding the identity of the artist who conceived and painted them.

❧❧❧

Reni's Archangel Michael

Angels abound throughout 17th and 18th-century art, and many famous artists painted various scenes depicting them. One of the most popular subjects, as well as the Annunciation, was the archangel Michael.

In 1636, the artist Guido Reni painted Michael trampling the head of Satan in a work that can now be seen in the Capuchin church of Santa Maria della Concezione in Rome. Reni

The Archangel Michael defeating Satan, Guido Reni, 1630.

was known for his skill and vision, but also for his unusual personal life. According to many reports, he had no sexual life whatsoever, and was so afraid of women that he believed he might be poisoned if he touched them. One story goes that he once discovered a woman's blouse that had been left by his laundress among his clothes, and became extremely fearful. His life of abstinence resulted in some extraordinary paintings, especially his later works, which are known for their meticulous, subtle harmonies and tones of colour.

Jacob and the Angel

Many artists have painted the biblical scene of Jacob wrestling with the angel. This story is told in *Genesis*, and later in the *Book of Hosea*. Depending on one's interpretation of the text, the angel could be Jacob himself (or his conscience), another man, or God. The angel calls himself Peniel, or Penuel, which is the name of the place where the fight takes place, as Jacob travels back to his homeland of Canaan.

In the biblical story, Jacob wrestles with the angel and overcomes him. During the fight, the angel tells him of his destiny, and his power to lead men in the name of God:

And Jacob was left alone; and there wrestled a man with him until the breaking of the day. And when he saw that he prevailed not against him, he touched the hollow of his thigh; and the hollow of Jacob's thigh was out of joint, as he wrestled with him. And he said, Let me go, for the day breaketh. And he said, I will not let thee go, except thou bless me. And he said unto him, What is thy name? And he said, Jacob. And he said, Thy name shall be called no more Jacob, but Israel: for as a prince hast thou power with God and with men, and hast prevailed.

This scene, which seems to allude to a very popular idea, that of wrestling with one's conscience or fate, has inspired a number of artists over the centuries. In 1659, Rembrandt painted the scene,

showing Jacob in hand-to-hand combat with the celestial being. In the 19th century, it was revived again in the work of the symbolists, surrealists, and visionary artists of the day.

Gustave Doré

The popular illustrator Gustave Doré made a famous etching of the scene in 1855, showing a serene yet powerful angel and a struggling Jacob; a similar pose inspired Eugene Delacroix in 1861, and Alexandre Louis Leloir in 1865, where the angel sports a very handsome pair of wings. Léon Bonnat, in 1876, gave the story another twist, with two handsome, muscular men, one an angel, one a mortal, locked in an almost erotic pose. The symbolist painter Gustave Moreau tackled the scene in 1878 with his own idiosyncratic take on classical and biblical mythology: in his painting, the angel appears to be completely unruffled and relaxed as Jacob does his best to make an impact. Even more strange is the painting by Paul Gauguin in 1888, also known as 'Vision after the Sermon'. Here, a group of Breton ladies in starched white bonnets look on dispassionately, as though at a bullfight, as the angel appears to vanquish Jacob, bending him over towards the ground.

Marc Chagall

In the 20th century, another notable version of the story can be seen in Marc Chagall's stained glass window at Fraumunster Abbey in Zurich. In 1940, Sir Jacob Epstein made a memorable sculpture of Jacob and the angel, in which the angel appears to hold the exhausted Jacob up, like a boxer after a fight. This illustrates the paradox of the biblical story, in which the angel wins, but tells Jacob that he has prevailed – showing, perhaps, that the person who struggles with their conscience, even if they feel they have been beaten, has won a victory through commitment to their cause.

The Angel of the North

The Angel of the North is a contemporary sculpture which has become a modern icon. The giant angel made of steel was designed by Antony Gormley and is situated in Gateshead, England, overlooking busy main roads and railways into Tyneside. It stands 66ft (20m) tall and has a wingspan of 174ft (54m). Because it is in such a windy spot, it has very solid foundations, consisting of 600 tonnes of concrete fixing it to the rock below. The steel, which is weather-resistant, was built in Hartlepool and weighs a massive 200 tonnes in all. The wings of the angel are angled at 3.5 degrees to give a protective feeling, as if the angel is in an embrace. Initially, its stark appearance caused controversy, but it has now become a well-loved feature of the landscape, and is viewed by an estimated 90,000 motorists each day. In 1998, it was decorated by football fans who put a shirt over it. It remained there for 20 minutes before the police arrived and took it down. The sculpture is known locally, and affectionately, as the 'Gateshead Flasher'.

Angel of the North, structure by Antony Gormley, Gateshead, England.

Banksy

In 2009, the artist Banksy showed his version of 'Angel of the North' – a classical sculpture of a young woman with wings and a halo. In keeping with his signature style of classical parodies, Banksy gave this very iconic image a 21st century update. She is wearing a tiny skirt and top and clutching her stilettos, presumably because they are too painful to wear after a night of dancing. The ground around her feet is littered with chips, takeaway boxes and a bottle. A cigarette is poking out between the fingers on her right hand, in which she is clutching a can. Though the sculpture is white, the angel's lips are painted with pink lipstick.

Everyday Angels

A number of artists in the 20th and 21st centuries have viewed angels as part of everyday life. Among these was Sir Stanley Spencer, who made it a habit to paint scenes from the Bible as if they were happening in his home town, a little place called Cookham on the River Thames. In his paintings, angels appear to well-known characters in the village, so that the stories from the Bible become immediate, up-to-date, and real.

In his lifetime, Spencer's most valued works were his intricate landscapes, but today he is best remembered for his surreal scenes, for example, of the Resurrection in 1924, which takes place in Cookham churchyard. His painting, *The Angel*, in 1953 shows the actual stone angel in the churchyard, with the church tower in the background.

Another British artist, Donald Pass, continues a tradition of visionary painting in England begun by William Blake in the 18th century. His works feature angels, often in heavenly choirs, and given an abstract sense of light and form. He reportedly began these paintings after experiencing a vision of the resurrection of the dead. One of his paintings shows the archangel Gabriel, with several pairs of wings, appearing in a red streak over a mass of human forms. Pass recounted that since the age of 12, he had seen visions of angels. In 1969, he visited a church in Sussex and saw a vision of the Resurrection in the grounds:

I was looking at a grave of a RAF pilot who was killed during the war and thinking how sad it was that someone should die so young, and suddenly everything went darker and darker and then it opened up. There was a vast landscape that went on and on. Tremendous lights appeared in the sky, and everything became quite different. Time did not matter. Then I began to see these lights coming towards me that appeared to be angels. There were masses of human figures and things like souls were rising from their bodies like something emerging from a chrysalis, something that was reborn. Some of these beings were standing nearby and some of them were collecting rising souls, and in the far, far distance there were some very dark figures. There was a tremendous sound of wind. A great angel appeared coming towards me and then there was a head, and all the light came from it. I could not see the faces of some of the beings at all; some had faces of lions, and others had a very mysterious feel about them. Eventually it all faded and I was looking at the grave again.

Angel of the North, by Banksy, 2009.

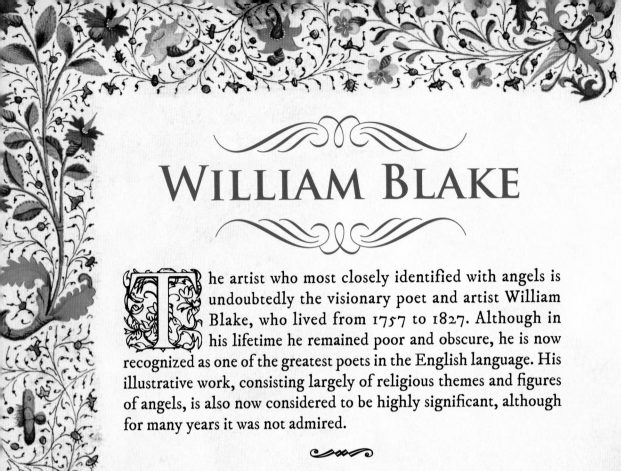

WILLIAM BLAKE

The artist who most closely identified with angels is undoubtedly the visionary poet and artist William Blake, who lived from 1757 to 1827. Although in his lifetime he remained poor and obscure, he is now recognized as one of the greatest poets in the English language. His illustrative work, consisting largely of religious themes and figures of angels, is also now considered to be highly significant, although for many years it was not admired.

'It is not because angels are holier than men or devils that makes them angels, but because they do not expect holiness from one another, but from God only.'

The artist who most closely identified with angels is undoubtedly the visionary poet and artist William Blake, who lived from 1757 to 1827. Although in his lifetime he remained poor and obscure, he is now recognized as one of the greatest poets in the English language. His illustrative work, consisting largely of religious themes and figures of angels, is also now considered to be highly significant, although for many years it was not admired.

Radical Thinker

William Blake lived most of his life in Soho, London, and travelled very little. As a child, his parents sent him to drawing classes and he educated himself in the classics, before becoming apprenticed to an engraver. He often visited Westminster Abbey to sketch, and it was there that he began to have visions of angels. Later, he exhibited at the Royal Academy and became part of a circle of radical thinkers and political activists. In 1782, he married Catherine Boucher, teaching her to read and write, and to help him in his engraving and illustrating work. She went on to become his devoted

companion, supporting him through many trials and tribulations, and assisting him in his day-to-day work as an illustrator.

A 'New Age'

Blake was a rebel, who was often in trouble with the authorities, and who disdained a conventional career. He believed that his own age was deeply lacking in spiritual values, and that a New Age was about to dawn, heralded only by prophetic visionaries such as himself. (The phrase 'New Age' was later borrowed from Blake to describe non-denominational religious spiritual movements in the 20th century).

Early in Blake's career, he began to illustrate religious themes, including passages from the Bible, often painting figures that he had seen in his visions. His illustrations were so strange and surreal that many contemporary critics thought him to be insane. One such illustration is *The Great Red Dragon and the Woman Clothed with the Sun* for the biblical *Book of Revelation*, showing an angel clothed in bright white light being hovered over by a demonic winged figure.

When Blake went on to show his work, his exhibitions were poorly attended and there were few reviews, most of them hostile. However, by the age of 65, when he began to work on a series of illustrations of the *Book of Job*, he began to attract some wealthy patrons, such as Thomas Butts, who admired his work. However, it was not until after his death that Blake was recognized as an important painter with a unique, complex vision of life, death, and the hereafter.

In the Company of Angels

Blake died, as he had lived, in the company of angels. Legend has it that on the day of his death, he was working on a series of illustrations for Dante's *Divine Comedy*. He stopped work, turned to his wife, and told her that he would draw her portrait, since she had been an angel to him throughout their marriage. He completed the portrait, which has since been lost, and then, in a kind of frenzy of joy, began to sing religious songs. A woman who was lodging in the house and attended his death bed later commented, 'I have been at the death, not of a man, but of a blessed angel.' After his death, Catherine reported that he visited her often from heaven, and at her own death, she remained calm and cheerful, calling out that she would soon be coming to meet him.

Blake's Angelic Visions

From an early age, Blake reported that he had experienced visions. At the age of four, he told his mother that he had seen, 'God put his head in the window'. At around 10, in Peckham Rye, London, he saw a tree full of angels, casting a bright light, and looking like stars. Legend has it that when he went home and reported his vision, his father tried to beat him for lying, and was only prevented from doing so by his mother. In another instance, he watched haymakers in a field, and saw angels walking among them. Although sometimes frustrated by his headstrong character, his parents were broadly supportive of him, helping him to translate his visions into real images by sending him to drawing school, rather than making him go through a conventional process of education.

Instructed by Archangels

Blake's visions continued throughout his life, and he attributed many of his paintings to them. He made no secret of the fact that he believed himself to be instructed by archangels to create his poems and artworks, so much so that some of his friends and admirers thought him to be losing his mind. The poet William Wordsworth wrote, 'There is no doubt that this poor man was mad, but there is something in the madness of this man which interests me more than the sanity of Lord Byron and Walter Scott'. This echoed the attitude of later generations after Blake's death: for a while he was dismissed as a lunatic, yet the critical, perceptive, and intellectual quality of his work shone through over time, and today he is hailed in some quarters as a genius of English literature and art.

Blake's Poem *The Angel*

One of Blake's poems, *The Angel*, characterizes his approach to the spiritual world. It is deceptively simple, employing no flowery phrases or long words. However, despite the simple language, the meaning of the poem remains somewhat mysterious:

> *I Dreamt a Dream! What can it mean?*
> *And that I was a maiden Queen*
> *Guarded by an Angel mild;*
> *Witless woe, was ne'er beguil'd!*
>
> *And I wept both night and day,*
> *And he wip'd my tears away;*
> *And I wept both day and night,*
> *And hid from him my hearts delight.*
>
> *So he took his wings and fled:*
> *Then the morn blush'd rosy red.*
> *I dried my tears and arm'd my fears,*
> *With ten thousand shields and spears.*
>
> *Soon my Angel came again;*
> *I was arm'd, he came in vain.*
> *For the time of youth was fled,*
> *And grey hairs were on my head.*

There might be many readings of this poem, but one may be that Blake is saying that we have access to grace and love if we care to take the opportunity to use these gifts from on high; however, very often, we 'arm our fears' and become defensive, and in this way lose contact with the spiritual world of the angels, rejecting the kindness, help, and support that they might be able to give us in our time of need.

Blake's Gallery of Angel Paintings

If there was one image that Blake painted over and over again, it was that of the angel. Running through his work, the icon of the angel constantly reappears. There are paintings of angels in almost every kind of pose; from the triumphant *Angel of Revelation* to the pair of angels praying over *Christ in the Sepulchre*, from the angels ascending and descending the stairs of *Jacob's Ladder* to the strange, multi-winged seraphim of *David Delivered Out of Many Waters*. Other fascinating and mysterious paintings include *The Good and Evil Angels*, in which the good angels holds a young child, shielding it from the threatening angel of death, and *Satan in his Original Glory*, showing Satan as he was before the fall, a beautiful multi-winged young man with a crown on his head, to which Blake added the subtitle, *Thou was Perfect until Iniquity was Found in Thee*. Another painting, *Satan Arousing the Rebel Angels* also shows Satan as a handsome young man; however, after the fall, in works such as *Satan Exulting over Eve*, the evil one is depicted in a more sinister light, with bat-like, reptilian wings, coloured a reddish brown.

Mystic, Visionary and Activist

In all Blake's angel paintings, we gain a sense of an artist engaged in a passionate quest for spiritual meaning. Although some of his images are strange and obscure, one gets the impression of a person with a purpose, to try to understand the celestial world that he believed to be part of the human experience. Although some of the paintings have a sense of being drawn from a private, personal vision – Blake often emphasized that he drew from his visions, and from the pictures he saw in his head – they are also based on his careful reading and radical interpretation of the scriptures. They also reveal his feelings about the real world around him, in 18th-century London, where poverty and misery was an everyday reality for thousands of people. In addition, because of his rebellious attitude towards the establishment, and his political activism, Blake sacrificed a successful career, and possibly fame and fortune, for his beliefs. Thus, today, we cannot dismiss Blake as a visionary with his head in the clouds; he was also a political thinker, and an intellectual, with a mission to try to communicate his belief in a 'new age' of redemption for humanity.

Blake's Legacy

After his death, Blake's work was forgotten for many years, but in the mid-19th century, after the publication of a biography by Alexander Gilchrist, he was taken up again by the school of painters known as the Pre-Raphaelites, including Dante Gabriel Rossetti and Algernon Swinburne. Like Blake, they shared a Romantic vision with a critical, radical attitude towards the society of the day. In the 20th century, Blake's reputation grew, and a number of scholars published books about him, leading to his influence among artists and writers such as the poet W.B. Yeats, who drew heavily on some of Blake's themes.

Later in the century, painters such as Paul Nash and Graham Sutherland showed their debt to Blake, as well as composers like Benjamin Britten and Vaughan Williams, who set some of his poems to music. Blake's work was also thought, by some commentators, to anticipate the ideas of Sigmund Freud and Carl Jung. In the 1950s, Blake went on to become a revered figure among the 'counter culture' beat poets such as Allen Ginsberg, also influencing a number of singers and songwriters including Bob Dylan. Today, Blake is recognized as one of the seminal figures of British culture, and as a precursor of many modern concepts, especially 'new age' thinking on such pressing issues as ecology.

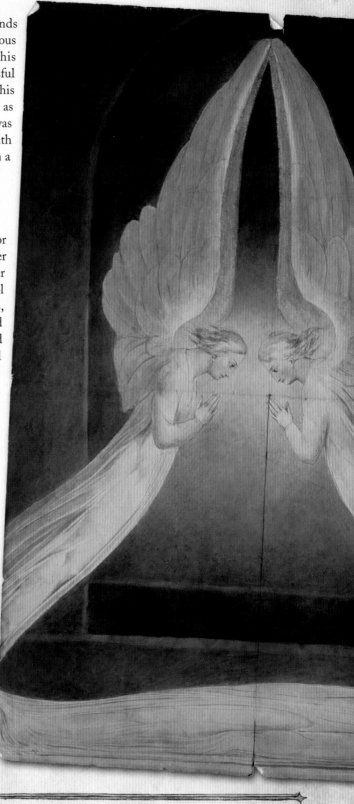

Christ in the Sepulchre, Guarded by Angels, William Blake, 1805.

PARADISE LOST

In modern times, many of our ideas about angels come from a major work in English literature: *Paradise Lost*, an epic poem in blank verse written by the poet John Milton and published in 1667. Most of the poem was written when Milton was completely blind, and dictated by him to his daughters, who transcribed it. Like the visionaries of the Bible, he claimed that a divine spirit visited him at night, leaving him with the verses, which he remembered in the morning.

Paradise Lost takes as its subject the epic creation story from the Bible, describing the temptation of Adam and Eve in the Garden of Eden, their fall from grace, and their expulsion from the garden. The villain of the story is Satan, the fallen angel, who tempts the first human beings in the guise of a serpent. Woven into the tale are Milton's views on the world he lived in, which included his radical political attitude towards the English civil war, which was raging at the time he was writing, and his profound spiritual beliefs. Although Milton draws on the New and Old Testament, he also uses material from the *Book of Enoch*, a religious text which is not part of the Bible. He was also familiar with Greek, Latin, and Hebrew, and used his knowledge of these languages to draw widely on his source material.

Satan, the Fallen Angel

At the time of writing *Paradise Lost*, Milton was poor and living in obscurity – some sources claim that he sold the copyright of the poem for just £10. Yet by the end of the century, it was considered to be one of the most important works in the English language, and continued to be published in many different editions in the centuries that followed.

Milton's imaginative retelling of the creation story gave his readers a new, much more morally complex reading of Christianity, by depicting heaven as a place in which a primal war breaks out between good and evil. He was particularly fascinated with the figure of Satan, the fallen angel, so much so that William Blake, who was much influenced by Milton, wrote:

'The reason Milton wrote in fetters when he wrote of Angels and God, and at liberty when of Devils and Hell, is because he was a true Poet and of the Devil's party without knowing it.'

Milton's Angels

In Milton's view, Christianity was not a set of edicts to be handed down by kings, bishops, and the established church. In keeping with his Protestant faith, he rather conceived of it as an intellectual and moral quest for faith and the possibility of human redemption in the face of suffering and despair. He continually emphasized the role of conscience in our lives and the personal nature of our relationship with God. The way he did this was to tell the creation story of the Bible as a story about angels – beings who are half divine, and half human.

In the view of some scholars, *Paradise Lost* is essentially a poem about angels. It is, in some of its parts, told by angels, and concerns the activities, conflicts, and communications of the heavenly messengers. The angels of Milton's story are real beings, and he tries to express their reasons for acting as they do in terms of their psychology and motivation. In many ways, Milton was creating a new concept of angels, moving more towards a Protestant view of angels as celestial beings who share many traits with humans, and away from the Catholic view of angels as entirely different in kind from mere mortals.

Satan and his Lieutenants

Paradise Lost tells two main stories: that of the Fall of Satan or Lucifer, and that of Adam and Eve. The story of Satan begins after God has cast him and his lieutenants, Mammon, Beelzebub, Belial, and Moloch, into hell. Satan volunteers to poison the newly created earth and embarks on many adventures in his attempt. He manages to trick Eve by taking advantage of her vanity; Adam follows suit, but is more knowingly a sinner than Eve. As a result of eating the fruit, lust enters into their relationship and they are banished by God from the Garden of Eden. However, the archangel Michael promises them that they will find a way to continue their relationship with God, albeit a more distant one.

Satan's Flaw

In the poem, Milton introduces Satan as a beautiful, talented young man. However, Satan's fatal flaw is that his ambition is too high: he wants to rule heaven, in place of God. Indeed, his pride

Portrait of John Milton, *c.*17th century.

is so important to him that he says, 'Better to reign in Hell than serve in Heaven'. He is a charismatic, persuasive person who manages to ingratiate himself to Eve by flattering her. He is also tremendously vain, with a massive ego that overpowers his occasional feelings of guilt at his trickery and deceit.

The Angel Raphael

Raphael's role in the story is to warn Adam about Satan's entry into the Garden of Eden, and Satan's desire to poison the happy relationship with God and each other that they are enjoying. Raphael talks to both Adam and Eve, but discusses Satan in private with Adam. Raphael tells Adam about the war in heaven, and Satan's expulsion into hell. Adam is shown as having an enquiring mind, so Raphael explains to him how the universe was created by God.

The Archangel Michael

As God's main military messenger, Michael's role is to escort Adam and Eve out of Eden, after they have gone against God's wishes and eaten from the Tree of Knowledge. Michael explains to Adam what the future for humanity holds, detailing the story of Cain and Abel, and then covering the main events of the Bible up to the advent of Jesus. Michael shows Adam that despite the sufferings of humanity, Jesus will eventually come to expel Satan, thus casting out evil, sin, and death from the world.

In Book Eleven of *Paradise Lost*, Adam tries to placate God by suggesting building an altar to worship him. He hopes that, in this way, he can persuade God to forgive him for his sin. Michael explains that this strategy will not work, because God does not approve of idolatry. He tells Adam that God is ever-present, and that humans do not need to build physical objects, whether altars or buildings, to worship him. Some critics have also argued that Milton saw Eve's vanity as a

form of idolatry, that is, she began to worship her own image rather than that of God. Much of *Paradise Lost* is an argument against the pomp and circumstance of the Catholic church, and an appeal to Christians to praise God in their everyday lives, without a great show of faith, but with real humility and devotion. Milton warns against placing too much faith in the Tree of Knowledge; while humans can learn great skills and gain much power through the quest for knowledge, it can never replace the simplicity, warmth, and love of a personal relationship with God.

The Angel Abdiel

In Milton's story, Abdiel is the only angel in Satan's host that stands up against the wickedness of his leader. It is Abdiel who brings the news of Satan's revolt to God, abandoning his master to perform a moral act. However, when he arrives, he finds God preparing for war. In the battle that takes place, Abdiel attacks Satan, and also rains blows on other angels, namely Ariel, Ramiel, and Arioch, as well as others. It has been speculated that Abdiel, as a sinner who repents, was a representation of Milton himself.

The Illustrators: from Medina to Doré

In the years that followed the publication of *Paradise Lost*, a number of talented artists illustrated the different editions of the poem, emphasizing the cosmic elements of the story. In the 17th century, it was illustrated by John Baptist Medina, who depicted the scenes in a Gothic, baroque style. Hosts of angels featured in nearly all of these illustrations, whether in the scenes of the Battle of Heaven, of the Expulsion from the Garden, or the Fall of Satan.

In the 18th century, Sir James Thornhill, Louis Cheron, Francis Hayman, and H. Richter emphasized the classical beauty of the subject matter, but Medina's more dramatic illustra-

Gustave Doré's illustration for John Milton's *Paradise Lost*, completed almost 200 years after its first publication.

tions proved more popular. The Swiss-born artist Henry Fuseli also made over 40 paintings of the story, and opened a gallery to display them in 1799. Like Medina's scenes, Fuseli's were full of massed angels in action poses, against a background of clouds and storms.

Gothic Horror

In 1804, William Blake produced a series of beautiful watercolour illustrations for *Paradise Lost*, but lack of public interest meant that he was forced to publish them himself. Much more popular were the illustrations by John Martin, who emphasized the grandiose nature of the scenes, especially in terms of the cosmic landscapes.

The Late Romantic artist, Gustave Dore, who shared with Martin a strong sense of Gothic horror and gloom, eventually became the most popular illustrator of the poem. Dore's illustrations showed angels and demons in highly stylized settings using an engraving technique that emphasized deep light and shade. His angels, led by Michael the archangel in gleaming armour, were bathed in glorious white light, with enormous feathered wings, while his demons, led by the shadowy figure of Satan, had scaly, reptilian, bat-like wings. Some critics felt that Dore's illustrations lacked subtlety and were too populist in style, caricaturing the drama of Milton's poem; however, while lacking respect in the art world, Dore's illustrations were very much admired by the general public, and he became a rich man.

The Legacy of Paradise Lost

The circumstances in which *Paradise Lost* was written has inspired a number of artists, including the 19th-century Romantic painter Eugene Delacroix. Delacroix painted a picture entitled, *Milton Dictating Paradise Lost to his Daughters*, showing the poet in a domestic setting, and emphasizing his blindness. In the 20th century, the artist Salvador Dali produced a set of 10 colour engravings inspired by *Paradise Lost*. These are dated 1974.

Painters and visual artists in general have been immensely inspired by *Paradise Lost*. In literature, its influence has been more widespread. Mary Shelley's *Frankenstein*, published in 1818, uses a quote from *Paradise Lost* at the beginning of the book, and cites it as one of the works the monster uses in his quest to become more human. In the 20th and 21st century, Philip Pullman's celebrated trilogy *His Dark Materials* takes its title from some lines of *Paradise Lost*:

Into this wild Abyss
The womb of Nature and perhaps her grave
Of neither sea, nor shore, nor air, nor fire
But all these in their pregnant causes mixed
Confusedly, and which thus must ever fight
Unless the Almighty Maker them ordain
His dark materials to create more worlds
Into this wild Abyss the wary Fiend
Stood on the brink of Hell and looked awhile
Pondering his voyage…

In Pullman's retelling of the story of *Paradise Lost*, the rebellion of the angels against God is seen as a triumph rather than a failure. In Pullman's view, one of humanity's greatest achievements has been to liberate itself from the oppressive nature of religion, and from the primitive belief, as he sees it, in a higher divinity. The novelist Salman Rushdie has also reworked ideas from *Paradise Lost* in *The Satanic Verses*, describing the fall from grace and redemption in terms that conflict with the original concept of Milton's story. Remarkably, it seems that Milton's fascination with Satan, and his attempt to portray him as a real flesh-and-blood human being, with strengths as well as weaknesses, has resulted in a more critical view of Christianity than he intended. Perhaps William Blake's remark, that Milton was of the devil's party without knowing it, may have come true in the new millennium, in the sense that *Paradise Lost* has inspired such important works as *His Dark Materials* and *The Satanic Verses*.

THE ANGEL CHURCH

Sculptures of angels adorn churches the world over. Angel imagery is such a common sight in churches, graveyards and memorials that we don't take much notice of it. Of course, some sculptures are so striking that they are hard to ignore. At Coventry Cathedral in the UK, a site famous for being heavily bombed in World War II, a large sculpture by artist Sir Jacob Epstein is attached to the wall by the main entrance. *Victory Over the Devil* depicts a triumphant looking St Michael, with arms and wings outstretched, resting a foot on the defeated Satan.

In the city of Vienna is one of the most beautiful sights, the Church of St Leopold (the 'Kirche am Steinhof'). The design of the church dates from the Art Nouveau period at the turn of the 19th century, and was built between 1903 and 1907 by the architect Otto Wagner. Also contributing to the project were sculptor Othmar Schimkowitz, who was responsible for the beautiful figures of angels guarding the church, and the artist Koloman Moser, who designed the mosaics and the stained glass in the building. Another sculptor, Richard Luksch, was employed to create the two sculptures of Austria's patron saints, Leopold and Severin, which look down from the two towers on either side of the entrance. The result of their joint labours was one of the most magnificent churches in the Art Nouveau style, which today is known as the 'angel church' because of the row of angels with gilded wings that line the roof of the central porch.

Healing Church

Situated on a hillside in the Penzing district of Vienna, the church stands over 300 metres above sea level. It was built as part of the Steinhof Psychiatric Hospital, which in those days was known by its full title of the Lower Austrian State Healing and Care Institution for the Neurologically and Mentally Sick. Because of this function as a place of worship for the infirm, the church has some quite unusual features: for example, there are emergency exits in various strategic places around the side walls, and the priest's area can be completely cordoned off, if necessary, from that of the congregation. This was so that, in the event of a patient becoming violent or needing to be removed promptly from the church, quick access to the area could be effected. In addition, the building and its furniture have few sharp edges, and most of the corner stones of the pillars are rounded off. In this way, carers could prevent the patients having accidents, or trying to damage themselves in any way during services.

There are also separate entrances in the church for male and female patients, who would have originally been segregated in the asylum. The confessional boxes within the interior are not entirely secluded, as they are in most Catholic churches. The church also boasts a number of easily accessible toilet facilities, which is another unusual feature. In the original church, pews were built to accommodate different types of patient, from those who could stand or sit calmly, to those who were disturbed and needed more space to move around. However, these have now been removed.

Flying Angels

As well as the angels standing guard over the entrance to the church, we find flying angels above the windows at the sides, which show images of saints. Also depicted is St Dymphna, the Irish patron saint of those who suffer from mental illness and disorders of the nervous system such as epilepsy. (St Dymphna is also responsible for those who work with the mentally ill, such as psychiatrists and nurses.) Sufferers from these conditions, and their carers, would have regularly been among the congregation in the days when the church was built.

The light in the church often attracts admiration, and in this respect, Otto Wagner, showed his great artistry and skill. Wagner, who was born in Penzing, was a follower of the school of 'architectural realism', which was more concerned with focusing on the day-to-day use of buildings than with classical form. He also advocated using modern materials to reflect the changing nature of society. When he designed the church, he evidently put his theories into practice; it is filled with light, and its construction shows how carefully he considered not only the physical needs of the patients who worshipped there, but their mental needs as well – for clear light, uplifting images, and a calming sense of beauty. Most visitors today are struck by this quality of the church; unlike many historic churches, it is not dark and gloomy, but filled with space and light, contrasting with the hustle and bustle of the city outside.

Tall, Elegant Angels

For many years, the church was allowed to fall into disrepair, but in 2006, after extensive renovation, it was reopened to the public. Today, masses and other services are held there, and the church seats a capacity of 800 people. As well as the elegant architecture of the church, the detailed mosaics and statuary inside it are in the finest art nouveau tradition. Koloman Moser, like Wagner a native of Vienna, was one of the great artists of the period, and for this project designed several stained glass windows, including one over the main entrance of the building, showing God seated on a throne, flanked by a pair of angels (these were the work of Othmar Schimkowitz).

The design was later used on a hundred-euro Austrian collector coin, the Steinhof Church commemorative coin, minted in November 2005. Perhaps the most immediately striking features of the church are the bronze angels by Schimkowitz, another major artist of the period. His angels are tall, slim, and with clean, elegant lines, unlike the baroque depictions of angels that were popular in Vienna at the time. As well as designing the angels for the church, Schimkowitz also designed a number of angels for the roof of the Austrian Postal Savings Bank in Vienna, working in conjunction with Wagner.

The Kirche am Steinhof is one of the great churches of Vienna, contrasting greatly with the rich style of the baroque to be found in many of its other religious and civic buildings. Its designers were members of the Vienna Secession, a group of artists headed by Gustav Klimt, who hoped to create art that was beautiful, modern, and functional, instead of being conservative, unwieldy, and old-fashioned, or constantly harking back to historical and outmoded forms. In the 'Angel Church' Otto Wagner, Koloman Kolo Moser, and Othmar Schimkowitz appear to have succeeded in their aim, to create a place of beauty, peace, tranquillity, and harmony for generations of visitors to the city, as well as for the mentally distressed patients and their carers living and working in the hospital.

Statues in front of the Kirche am Steinhof, Austria.

ANGELS IN FICTION

ANGELS IN LITERATURE

Angels are extremely popular figures in fiction. Being the embodiment of inspiration themselves it is no surprise that they have appeared in works across all mediums; but it is in books that the self-help angel can sit alongside the fictional.

Angel Fiction

Queen of the vampire fiction genre Anne Rice made a transition to the more heavenly side of the supernatural world and wrote a two-part series on angels. *Songs of the Seraphim* includes part one: *Angel Time*, which was released in 2009 and part two: *Of Love and Evil*, which was released in 2010. The books follow Toby O'Dare, a former government assassin who is called upon by angels to solve a sinister crime but gets caught up in a series of dark plots that he must unravel. On the lighter end of the angel fiction spectrum are fantasy titles which appeal to a young adult market. In the 2009 novel *Hush Hush* by Becca Fitzgerald, a high school student becomes romantically involved with a mysterious newcomer at her school, only to discover that he is a fallen angel, and their relationship is putting her in danger. In the same year, Lauren Kate published her novel *Fallen*, a story about Lucinda, a girl who starts a new school and becomes strongly attracted to a boy named Daniel Grigori. She feels as though she has met Daniel before, and despite his constant scowls at her, she remains interested in him. She then meets a new love interest, 'good guy' Cam, and has to decide between the pair. Lucinda begins to delve into Daniel's secretive past and uncovers a book about fallen angels, ostensibly written by an ancestor of Daniel Grigori. *Fallen* is the first installment in the four-piece series and looks set to be adapted to the big screen. Taking a departure from the 'star-crossed lovers at high school formula' is the novel

Going Bovine by Libby Bray, also published in 2009. Cameron is a slacker student who contracts mad cow disease which, he is told, he will eventually die of. As a result he is visited by Dulcie, a pink-haired angel with spray-painted wings. She informs him that an elusive physicist who travels through time, Dr X, can help him, but they must track him down. He then goes on an adventure, encountering fire-breathing dragons while being pursued by the Wizard of Reckoning. The clever twist on this story is that the reader is unsure whether Cameron is physically taking this journey, or if it is a product of his disease and just in his imagination.

Angels In My Hair

In literature, certain angel clichés are kept to. Though the angels of the youth fantasy genre are adapted to appeal to their target audience, traditionally, in fiction, they adhere to the basic rules.

They always have wings, though some choose to keep them hidden until the right moment calls for them to be revealed. They are usually female, wearing white, diaphanous robes. An ethereal glow surrounds them, and their presence oozes light and tranquility. Their role is messenger; popping up to guide and help mere mortals in their hour of need. To some authors, however, they are not fictional beings, but real-life constant companions. Author Lorna Byrne has been seeing angels since she was a little girl and decided to share her experiences with the world. Her 336-page autobiographical book entitled *Angels in my Hair* details her life growing up surrounded by angels, and how she still uses them to this day for inspiration and guidance. Despite attracting a lot of cynicism at first, the book triumphed and has been translated into 21 languages and sold in 47 countries.

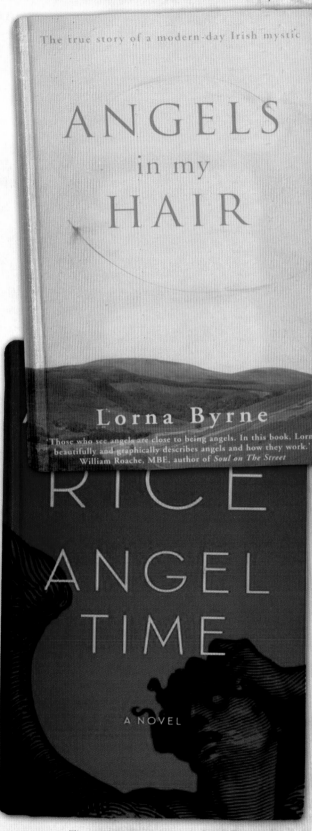

The novels *Angels in my Hair* by Lorna Byrne and *Angel Time* by Anne Rice.

ANGELS ON
SCREEN

 ngels are a rich source of inspiration to writers, but it is through the mediums of television and film that the angel really comes to life.

ANGELS AT THE MOVIES

The screen angel is often on a mission from God to help the living, sometimes with the incentive of earning his or her wings back and ascending back to heaven, much like in *It's a Wonderful Life* and *Highway to Heaven*. In the cases of *Dogma*, the angel Metatron and his friends are charged with the task of preventing an Apocalypse, and in *Legion*, archangel Michael fights against God's commands to start one. The angel is a powerful figure and sometimes very charming. In *The Bishop's Wife*, the angel played by Cary Grant becomes enamoured with the wife of the bishop he is trying to help, and in *City of Angels*, Meg Ryan's human character ends up falling in love with Nicolas Cage's angel character, Seth.

It's a Wonderful Life, 1946

Directed by Frank Capra, it stars James Stewart, and tells the story of a man named George Bailey, who, in a fit of depression, tries to kill himself on Christmas Eve – only to alert his guardian angel to his plight.

News of George's predicament has reaches heaven, so Clarence Odbody, an angel in training (played by Henry Travers), is dispatched down to earth to earn his wings by helping him. Clarence introduces himself as George's guardian angel, but – not

Film poster for *It's a Wonderful Life*, directed by Frank Capra, 1946.

surprisingly – George doesn't believe him. So Clarence sets about showing George that his life is meaningful, by revealing what would have happened to his family, friends, and community had he not lived. Reviewing his life thus, George finds that there are many people he has helped, including several whose lives he has saved; he also realizes that he is part of a close-knit community, which will be devastated if he kills himself.

The film was a box-office flop when it was released. It was nominated for several Oscars, but failed to win any. However, it has since become a classic, and is often shown on television at Christmas time. With its feel-good, positive message of community values and common kindness, together with its appealing wit and humour, it is seen today as one of the most inspiring films to come out of the period.

Angel on my Shoulder, 1946

In the same year, another angel-themed, but very different, film appeared: *Angel on My Shoulder*, directed by Archie Mayo. It was a fantasy film about gangsters, and told the story of Eddie Kagle, who is killed by his childhood friend and partner in crime Smiley Williams. Kagle descends into hell, where Old Nick tells him that he can return to earth in the body of a judge, Frederick Parker, and kill Smiley in revenge. As the judge, Kagle does his best to be evil, but somehow he never pulls it off. In the process, he falls in love with the judge's girlfriend, and changes his view of life. When his chance comes to kill Smiley, he does not take it.

The Bishop's Wife, 1947

Romantic comedy *The Bishop's Wife* follows the story of an angel coming to Earth to help a recently appointed bishop (David Niven) with his problems. Bishop Henry Broughman is tasked with the duty of raising funds to build a new cathedral, and he becomes so preoccupied with this

mission that he starts to neglect his wife, Julia, and daughter, Debbie. When the bishop prays for help it arrives in the form of an angel, played by the charismatic and charming Cary Grant, who is more interested in flirting with Julia than helping the bishop. In 1996 a similarly-named version, *The Preacher's Wife*, was released starring Denzel Washington and Whitney Houston. It was not as well received as the original, but the two films remain classic angel pictures.

Angels in the Outfield, 1951

This black-and-white film starred Paul Douglas and Janet Leigh, and was directed by Clarence Brown. Set in the world of baseball, it tells the story of one Guffy McGovern, a hard-bitten manager, who hears an angel call to him one night. The angel, as it transpires, is the leader of a heavenly team of dead baseball players, and offers to help McGovern's team, the Pittsburg Pirates, on the condition that they start to behave more decorously, eschewing their normal habits of fighting and swearing. The angels go on to help the team, but a child, Bridget White, who has prayed to the archangel Gabriel, is able to see their presence on the field. Soon, newspaper reports about the phenomenon emerge, and the plot thickens; however, all ends happily. Loved by baseball aficionados for its realism, *Angels on the Outfield* was also memorable for the fact that the audience never actually saw the angels, but their supernatural presence was hinted at. It was remade in 1994, starring Danny Glover, Tony Danza, and Christopher Lloyd, but did not achieve the success of the original.

Barbarella, 1968

The sci-fi movie *Barbarella*, starred a scantily clad Jane Fonda in the title role, and featured a handsome, tanned, blond angel, Pygar, who is blind and who has lost his will to fly. Pygar comes to the heroine's rescue when she is knocked unconscious by a rockslide. Having come to her aid on numerous occasions during her adventures, Barbarella shows her gratitude by making love to the angel, and he responds by becoming able to fly once more. He also utters the immortal line, 'An angel does not make love, an angel is love'. Pygar then helps Barbarella continue on her quest by flying her to various places in the universe. Despite its tongue-in-cheek humour and imaginative setting, the film was not well received on its release, though it has since gained a cult following.

Heaven Can Wait, 1978

Warren Beatty was the star and director of this classic angel movie. The plot revolves around an over-zealous guardian angel, who takes a football player, Joe Pendleton, up to heaven after an accident, before he has actually died. Once in heaven, Joe discovers he should not be there at all, since he was not due to die yet, but as his body has already been cremated, he is forced to inhabit a new one, that of millionaire Leo Farnsworth, who has been murdered by his wife Julia. Joe returns to earth, and a succession of comic complications ensue, ending with Joe falling in love with Betty Logan, played by Julie Christie.

Film poster, *Heaven Can Wait*, directed by
Warren Beatty, 1978.

Wings of Desire, 1987 and City of Angels, 1998

The following decade produced the memorable *Wings of Desire*, directed by Wim Wenders and released in 1987. Inspired by the poetry of Rainer Maria Rilke, the story concerns two angels, Damiel and Cassiel, played by Bruno Ganz and Otto Sander respectively, as they walk around Berlin, observing the unhappiness of those around them. Instead of going to their aid, they are simply there to pay their respects to humanity, recording and witnessing what is going on. As the film progresses, Damiel falls in love with a circus performer named Marion, and decides to abandon his spiritual form for life as a human being, experiencing the joys and sorrows of physical existence for the first time. Meanwhile, Cassiel tries but fails to prevent a young man killing himself by jumping off a high building. At the end of the film, Damiel and Marion become lovers. The film was a critical success, and continues to remain a cinema classic. In 1998, a remake directed by Brad Siberling entitled *City of Angels* was released. Set in Los Angeles, it follows two angels Seth (Nicholas Cage) and Cassiel (Andre Braugher) as they carry out their mission of guiding those that are near death into their next life. Seth and Cassiel often speak to the nearly deceased about their favourite times in life, but despite this contact in a person's darkest hour, they do not understand humans and cannot relate to their feelings. One day, Seth is at a hospital, at the side of a patient undergoing heart surgery. Maggie (Meg Ryan) is trying valiantly to save the man's life, and when she cannot, she is devastated. This display of humanity catches Seth's attention and he becomes preoccupied by her. Later, he decides to take on human form, and therefore become visible, so he can befriend her. Their friendship is flawed as Seth cannot reveal many details about his background to her, but despite this, and the fact that Maggie is dating a colleague, a

mutual attraction develops. Seth meets Nathaniel Messinger, one of Maggie's patients. Nathaniel reveals that he was once an angel, and that he became human permanently through the process of 'falling'. Seth considers doing this so he can have a normal relationship with Maggie, just as her colleague proposes to her, leaving her having to choose between the two men. Later, Maggie realizes that Seth is invulnerable to injuries, and dwells on how little she really knows about him. She asks him what he is and when he tells her, she cannot accept the truth. She later confides in Nathaniel, who tells her about his angelic past, and the reasons he became a human. He tells her that Seth is thinking of doing the same for her, giving up his position in heaven to be with her on earth. Meanwhile, Seth has made the decision to do it, and leaps from a tall building. As soon as he wakes up he begins to feel human sensations for the first time. He is in intense pain and, his personality now changed completely, is desperate to find Maggie. Somehow he gets to the hospital, only to be told she has gone to her uncle's mountain cabin in Lake Tahoe. He resolves to get there, but due to his naivety he gets mugged and his boots stolen. He manages to hitch a lift to the cabin, and arrives on her doorstep, soaking wet and shivering. She sees his breath in the night air and realizes that he has made the ultimate sacrifice for her, and they are finally together physically. The next day, Seth is taking a shower while Maggie heads out to the store on her bike. As she rides along she is overcome with joy; she shuts her eyes and flings her arms out, when suddenly she is hit by a truck. Seth senses that something has happened to her and rushes to her aid. Maggie tells Seth that she can see angels and that they have come to take her away. Seth, since becoming a human, can no longer see the angels but he knows they are there. She tells him that when they ask her what her favourite thing is, she will say it was him. Time passes and Seth is now alone and grieving for Maggie. Cassiel visits him and offers him comfort, and Seth says

Artwork from the film *City of Angels*, directed by Brad Silberling, 1998.

that becoming a human was worth it for the short time he had with Maggie. Though it takes Seth some time to adjust to his new life, in the final scene on the beach, surrounded by angels, he runs into the water and is bursting with joy at being a human.

The Prophecy, 1995

The Prophecy, entitled *God's Army* in Europe, is a horror movie starred Christopher Walken, and tells the story of archangel Gabriel and a police detective who becomes embroiled in a celestial war. The movie was extremely successful, spawning four sequels.

Michael, 1996

John Travolta stars as archangel Michael whose behaviour is anything but angelic. He comes to the attention of tabloid editor Vartan Malt (Bob Hoskins) who is always on the look out for ridiculous and scandalous stories to boost his sales. When Vartan hears that a woman in Iowa is living with an angel, he sends out three people to investigate: Dorothy Winters (Andie McDowell), a so-called angel expert, Huey Driscoll (Robert Pastorelli), a photographer and Frank Quilan (William Hurt), a reported whose career is going down the pan. The trio arrive at the home of Pansy Millbank (Jean Stapleton) who surprises them all by admitting that her tenant is an angel and readily introduces them to him. Although he has wings, they soon realize that he is nothing like an angel. He has a pot belly from his addiction to sweet foods, has poor personal hygiene, he chain-smokes, drinks and uses foul language. Michael explains to the journalists that angels are allowed to take holidays, and he is in the middle of the last one he will ever be allowed to take. Later, and after the unexpected death of Pansy, Frank and Huey have an idea. They suggest that they take Michael to Chicago, so he can really let loose on his final holiday. On the way to Chicago

it is revealed that Michael is really on a mission during his time on Earth, and that was to make Dorothy and Frank fall in love. The character of the lustful, drunken Michael was undoubtedly influenced by depictions of Michael in the 1973 play by British playwright Dennis Potter, *Angels are So Few*. The representation of the archangel Michael here is rather an unorthodox one. The fact that he smokes and drinks, and apparently smells of cookies, are typical of an unhealthy lifestyle, and not what is considered to be angelic. Of course, Michael explains that he is on holiday, so perhaps he is simply indulging on earthly vices while he has the chance. Michael's wings are large, almost comically so, and they occasionally molt. Despite his disheveled appearance he stays true to his angelic mission, and through the course of the film performs a minor miracle and imparts unexpected pearls of wisdom.

A Life Less Ordinary, 1997

From Heaven, angels are responsible for making humans fall in love and live happily ever after. Angel partners O'Reilly (Holly Hunter) and Jackson (Delroy Lindo) haven't been performing very well of late and the 'Captain' Gabriel (Dan Hedaya) decides to introduce an incentive. He charges O'Reilly and Jackson with the mission of making American millionaire (Cameron Diaz) fall in love with Scottish cleaner (Ewan McGregor). If they do not succeed with this mission, they must spend eternity on Earth.

Dogma, 1999

Kevin Smith's 1999 comedy *Dogma* features an all-star cast playing a host of heavenly characters. Ben Affleck and Matt Damon play two fallen angels, Bartleby and Loki, who get expelled from heaven by God and exiled to Wisconsin, USA. The pair want to get back to heaven and know that the only way they can do so would be by finding a loophole in Catholic dogma. The perfect opportunity presents itself when they hear that the Red Bank church in New Jersey is celebrating its anniversary with a plenary indulgence. They realize that if they pass through the doors of the church their sins will be forgiven, and when they die, they will be allowed back into heaven. What they haven't realized though is that to overrule the word of God would destroy all of existence, something that seraph Metatron (Alan Rickman) must try and prevent happening. Metatron, as the voice of God, appears to mere mortal Bethany (Lina Fiorentino) in her sleep and charges her with the mission of stopping Loki and Bartleby. She, having lost her faith in God, declines the mission. The next day she is met my two unlikely prophets, Jay and Silent Bob, who save her from an attack by the Stygian Triplets, an evil trio sent from hell to kill her. Metatron had revealed to her that she would meet the prophets, and it is then that she begins to take her mission seriously. Soon she meets Rufus (Chris Rock), the 13th

apostle who never made it into the Bible due to being black, and Serendipity (Salma Hayek), a muse. As the film progresses, Bethany discovers the reason she was chosen for this mission, she is the last Scion, the last living relative of Mary and Joseph and so it is her duty to stop Loki and Bartleby succeeding in their plan. Metatron explains that sometimes God takes human form and goes to Earth to play skee ball, and that he had not returned from his last trip. He goes on to explain that God is most likely still on Earth, but in such a bad state that he cannot get back to heaven.

They arrive at the Red Bank church and try to convince Cardinal Glick to cancel the plenary indulgence, but he refuses. At a nearby bar, exiled muse Arzael (Jason Lee) is holding Bethany and friends hostage. He explains that he is behind the fallen angels' plan, and that he is determined to let them destroy all of existence so he will not have to spend eternity in hell. Rufus manages to

Artwork from the film *Dogma*, directed by Kevin Smith, 1999.

kill Azrael with a golf club he had stolen from Cardinal Glick's office, counting on the fact that the club would have been blessed by Glick. They arrive at the church to discover Bartleby and Loki have been massacring innocent people. The fallen angels are preparing to walk through the church doors but are stopped by the gang. Meanwhile Bethany and Silent Bob race to a local hospital convinced that a comatose patient there is God in human form. Bethany removes the life support and God escapes, killing her as a martyr. At the church, Loki has been killed by Bartleby after he was turned human when his wings were severed. God arrives at the scene, in Her human form. Bartleby, now full of remorse for his actions, is approached by God, who uses the power of Her voice to kill him. Silent Bob carries Bethany's corpse and places it before God, who then uses Her omnipotence to bring her back to life. All the celestial characters then walk through the church doors and return to heaven.

Dogma features many biblical characters and the overall uniqueness of the film comes from how it represents these figures, which is largely very different to most 'angel films'. Here, Metatron, aka the voice of God, is a sarcastic character who has little patience for idiots. The prophets, who spend more time stoned than foretelling the future, appear less than holy. Jay is the foul-mouthed deviant half of the duo, whereas Silent Bob is a dubious character, though he does have slightly more integrity than Jay. God is portrayed as someone who, despite having all of creation and limitless power at 'his' divine fingertips, makes occasional trips to earth to play American arcade game skee ball. When doing this, God takes the form of a middle-age man, but as is revealed at the end of the film, God's true form is female – something that Bethany makes clear she suspects a few times throughout *Dogma*.

Artwork from the film *Legion*, directed by Scott Stewart, 2010.

Constantine, 2005

Keanu Reeves stars as detective, and demon hunter, Jonathan Constantine in this action/fantasy/thriller film. Policewoman Angela Dodson teams up with the otherworldly Constantine to help solve the mystery behind her twin sister's suicide, as Angela refuses to believe that her sister, as a Catholic, would take her own life. The investigation leads the pair into the underworld of demons and angels that exists beneath Los Angeles, and Constantine uncovers that demons are trying to enter the human realm. Through this discovery he ends up in a battle with Satan himself.

Legion, 2010

Legion is a supernatural thriller starring Paul Bettany and Dennis Quaid. When God loses faith in humanity, he commands Archangel Michael and a legion of angels to go to earth and bring on the Apocalypse, ultimately wiping out the human race. Michael lands in Los Angeles and rebels against God's wishes, finding himself holed up in a roadside diner with a waitress who is pregnant with the messiah. The film did not do very well at the box office and attracted a lot of criticism due to its depiction of the nature of God and angels.

ANGELS IN TELEVISION

Highway to Heaven, 1984-1989

The NBC classic *Highway to Heaven* starred Michael Landon as Jonathan Smith, an angel sent down to Earth by God aka 'the Boss'. He is accompanied by a human, named Mark Gordon, played by Victor French. Jonathan is on earth as a term of his 'probation', and his mission is to help people overcome their issues. If he successfully helps enough people he will earn his wings and ascend back to heaven. Jonathan and Mark become very good friends despite their massive differences, and the threat that Jonathan may suddenly be sent back to heaven concerns Mark, who would rather his buddy stayed with him.

Touched by an Angel, 1994-2003

American television show *Touched by an Angel* ran for an impressive 211 episodes during its 9 seasons, and has come to be regarded as a classic. The concept of the show was very similar to *Highway to Heaven*, with the plot revolving around angels being sent to provide guidance to mortals, under the ultimate supervision of God. Monica (Roma Downey) is an angel working underneath Tess (Della Reese), their mission is to attend to people who are faced with problems or hard decisions; they refer to these missions as 'cases'. When called to a case, they then pass on the advice of God, and lead the problem to resolution. Each episode deals with a different case and as the series goes on Monica progresses from caseworker to supervisor. Whenever an angel reveals its true identity to a mortal, the angel becomes bathed in a heavenly glow.

Angels in America, 2003

HBO miniseries *Angels in America* is adapted from a play by Tony Kushner, who earned a Pulitzer Prize for his work. Kushner adapted the play for television and Mike Nichols directed. *Angels in America* is set in 1985 and follows the failing relationships of Prior Walter and Louis Ironson, and Joe and Harper Pitt. These interconnecting relationships are set against two major backdrops: the Reagan administration and the AIDS epidemic of the mid-1980s, with two characters, Prior and Roy, suffering from the disease. Emma Thompson stars as the Angel of America, a figure which appears to Prior many times, insisting that he is a prophet, and Meryl Streep appears as the Angel of Australia. The appearance of these angels is rather stereotypical;

they have long flowing locks, wear diaphanous robes and their wings are impressively big and covered in pure white feathers.

Supernatural, 2005-present

In the fourth season of the Warner Bros show *Supernatural*, the writers decided to add a Christian mythology theme into the drama and horror mix, and so they introduced a few angels and archangels. These figures inhabit a human vessel on Earth, as beholding an angel's true form can be fatal to humans. Their wings are never seen, though references to them are made, including one occasion where a shadow of angel Castiel's wings are seen. The angel Zachariah reveals that in his true form he has six wings (perhaps an indication of angelic rank) and four faces, one of which is a lion. The physical size of an angel is believed to be huge, with Castiel once comparing his height to New York's Chrysler Building. Initially, Anna, an angel, claims that angels have no emotions or free will. However, as the drama unfolds from season to season, the angels display many feelings of loyalty and affection. They refer to each other as siblings and to God as their father, although Anna says that only four angels (implied to be the archangels) have ever seen God in his true form.

The angels and archangels have many powers

Artwork from the television mini series *Angels in America*, directed by Mike Nichols, 2003.

and abilities. The archangels share the abilities of the regular angels, though to a much higher level, and have extra powers in addition to the shared ones. The strength of the powers the angels possess slowly diminish in accordance with the length of time they have spent out of heaven – it is not said whether this rule applies to the archangels too. The following are powers shared by both angels and archangels:

ANGELIC POSSESSION: Angels have the ability to possess a human 'host'. They need the human's permission before they do this, unlike the demons of *Supernatural*.

INVULNERABILITY: Due to their high tolerance for physical pain and their advanced immune system, angels are impervious to contracting disease, suffering from an illness or sustaining injury. This invulnerability is a product of the combined human vessel and celestial host. However, they are able to become inebriated if they consume a quantity of alcohol so high that it would kill a mere mortal.

KILLING TOUCH: This power is used to defeat demons and works by an angel placing a hand on the demon's forehead, killing it instantly.

MEMORY MANIPULATION: A human's memory can be tampered with by an angel, as they are able to remove and restore certain memories. They can also plant fake memories inside a human's mind.

SEDATION: A human can be temporarily sedated if an angel places two fingers on his/her forehead.

SUPER STRENGTH: The angels can tune into the human strength within the vessel that they inhabit, and enhance it using their own powers. The result is a strength which can cause immense harm to humans.

TELEKINESIS: Using their minds, angels are able to move or throw objects. The more experienced can also break a human's bones, should they need to.

TELEPATHY: The angels have the ability to read each others minds, and those around them. They can also enter the dreams of humans.

TELEPORTATION: Angels can teleport anywhere, and the sound of their wings flapping can be heard when they do this. They can teleport others with them, and also teleport others without visiting the desired location too.

꙰

Saving Grace, 2007–2010

American crime drama series *Saving Grace* follows the life of detective Grace Hanadarko (Holly Hunter) in Oklahoma City. Grace leads an interesting lifestyle for an agent of the law. She drinks a lot, smokes and is rather promiscuous. The series opens with Grace drink-driving her Porsche and running down and killing a pedestrian. She gets out of her car and realizes what she's done, before collapsing to the floor and screaming out to God for help. Suddenly, a scruffily-dressed man appears, chewing tobacco. He introduces himself as Earl and unfolds his wings; Grace realizes she is in the presence of an angel. Earl tells her that because of what she has done, she will be going to hell unless she turns her life around and follows God. When Earl disappears, Grace is shocked to discover the corpse has vanished too, and it seems as if the accident never happened. She notices a small amount of blood on her blouse and so takes it to her forensics expert at the police station. Rhetta Rodriguez (San Giacomo) analyzes the blood and determines that it belongs to a prisoner on death row, Leon Cooley (Bokeem Woodbine), who gets visited by Earl regularly. As the series progresses Earl appears to Grace many more times, urging her to get off the path of self-destruction. An interesting aspect of *Saving Grace* is that it does not promote or support any single religion. The issue here is faith, and how faith can be the hardest thing to keep in the modern world. Earl is similar in appearance to John Travolta's character in *Michael*. This idea hints that angels can appear to us in many forms, and that the popular perception of them may be wholly inaccurate.

Our Lady of the Harbour, statue situated
atop a church in Quebec, Canada

INDEX